THE UNCENSORED
JOHN HENRY FAULK

THE UNCENSORED
JOHN HENRY FAULK

by John Henry Faulk

Foreword by LOUIS NIZER

TexasMonthlyPress

Texas Monthly Press, Inc.
P.O. Box 1569
Austin, Texas 78767

A   B   C   D   E   F   G   H

Library of Congress Cataloging in Publication Data

Faulk, John Henry.
    The uncensored John Henry Faulk.

    I. Title.
PS3556.A92U5   1985   818'.5409   84-24051
ISBN 0-87719-013-5

To Yo and Liz

Contents

Foreword

Faulk's activities have scanned a wide range of serious subjects, from recording and thus preserving the black preachers' sermons, whose imaginative interpretations of the Bible are sheer art, to his struggle in the courts to strike down McCarthyism and blacklisting on television.

He is chiefly known as a homespun philosopher and humorist. His predecessors were Will Rogers, Mark Twain, Robert Benchley, Finley Peters Dunne (Dooley), Kim Hubbard, George Ade, Harry Herschfield, and many others.

It is in the great American tradition to choose a humorist by popular choice and make him the folk hero of his generation. He tells us the truth about our leaders and ourselves, without offending us.

Satire is a delectable skin for the luscious fruit within. Faulk is a masterful exponent of this art. To hear him tell about the Republican (and now Democrat) who is fed and kept on a reservation in a Texas state park in order to preserve a disappearing species, or to hear him argue that Congress ought to be impeached instead of Nixon, is to get a glimpse into the humorous world, which fundamentally is sad.

Yet it was John Henry Faulk, the provocateur of humor, who found himself in a disturbing personal dilemma — he became the victim of a libel. Then he demonstrated his fortitude with doggedness and sacrifice as he fought against great odds to be vindicated. A jury did so. There was no humor in that fight — it was a heroic achievement for justice.

Now readers are given the opportunity to have a kaleidoscopic view of a man who pursued his many talents through humor until destiny required him to wage a libel suit that was to wipe out blacklisting in the television industry. Readers may therefore expect to take a roller-coaster ride, screaming with laughter and joy and then, on the descent, with fear. This book ensures an exhilarating experience.

Louis Nizer

Acknowledgments

Much of the material in this book was created over a long stretch of years, so it's nigh on to impossible to acknowledge all those to whom I am indebted. However, there are a number of hearty souls to whom I owe special thanks. There is good Angus Cameron, now retired, whom J. Frank Dobie called the most ample mind in publishing. He early on urged me to write this book. And there is Alan Lomax, lifelong friend and inspirer, who perceived value in much of the material I produced even before I did. Cactus Pryor has always been a willing aide in polishing up my work. Jubal R. Parten, that great friend of all that is enlightened and worthwhile in Texas, let me in on his ruminations about how this republic is faring, always to my considerable advantage. Mary Ann Crossley, who helped select and edit material with tireless dedication and great professional skill, has my heartfelt gratitude. To that stalwart Frank Dyer of Houston for his advice and perceptive criticism. Don Carleton, out at the Barker Library at the University of Texas at Austin, has been a valued assistant in that area too. His cooperation has been beyond reckoning, as has been the goodwill and help of Scott Lubeck. The person to whom I owe the most, of course, and without whom this book would never have come into being, is my keenest critic and most helpful assistant, Elizabeth Peake Faulk, my wife.

I
On Humor

I

In a reminiscence on the development of his unique style of humor, John Henry Faulk draws a poignant picture of growing up in a Texas community that was half southern, half western. The central conflict is his love of the people he knows versus alienation from the repression and bigotry of small-town American life. How could he state his own views and still be accepted in his hometown? Faulk's solution was to turn to humor as a social weapon, whether imitating the Ladies' Missionary Society outside his mother's window or turning the tables on a local bigot at the hardware store. Though his mother wished him to be a Methodist minister, Faulk's pulpit was on the stage, not in the church. By the time he reached young adulthood, he had joined the American tradition whereby we tolerate and even embrace the critic who tells us how absurd we are: the humorist.

This treatise on American humor also reveals Faulk's singular contribution to that tradition. Instead of basing his wit on jokes or one-line witticisms, Faulk's approach is to create a folk character who slowly spins a whole world of attitudes and contradictions at which we all laugh, sometimes gently, sometimes bitterly. The combination of vernacular regional speech and sharp wit is the special Faulk hallmark.

As nearly as I can tell, my particular brand of humor is the result of my mother's misdirected prayers. Some months before I was born, my mother was seized with the strong desire that I be a boy so she could dedicate my life to what she considered the highest calling any human being could achieve in this life: the Methodist ministry.

My mother was fairly tolerant of other sects and religions. She was convinced, however, that the Lord put most of His faith in the Methodist church—specifically the Southern Methodist Church, Texas style. Methodist preachers were His favorite, most dependable messengers on Earth.

"You were born," my mother told me, "a little dumpling of a boy, and I was convinced the Lord had answered my prayers. It wasn't until a few years later that I realized I had drawn a blank."

"How old was I when you realized I wasn't cut out to be a Methodist preacher, Mama?" I asked.

"I don't remember, exactly," she replied, "whether it was by the time you learned to walk or by the time you learned to talk. But I do remember this: by the time you were six years old the kind of words you were using and the way you played fast and loose with the truth caused me to forget the Methodist ministry and switch prayers. I started promising the Lord that if he would just keep you out of the state penitentiary I would settle for you being anything."

There you have the dilemma that shaped my life: while my mother was praying for me to go into the Methodist ministry, my attitude and conduct turned me in a different direction from my tenderest years onward.

One of the peculiar practices the good Methodists in our community employed to assure their children a head start to glory was to avoid absolutely any mention of matters relating to sex. This included responding to children's questions about human birth with the firm statement: "The stork brings babies."

This patent nonsense was believed by all the children in my peer group, including me. Including me, that is, until one sunny morning in May when I was about eight years old. My constant companion at that time was Snooky Bates, one of the many children of a black family who lived near our place and worked on my father's farm.

Snooky Bates and I were sitting on a fence out at the cow lot observing the birth of a calf. The sight was old hat to both of us. We had seen calves, puppies, kittens, and pigs arriving quite often.

The sight of the emerging calf prompted Snooky to remark, quite casually, that he and I had arrived in this world by roughly the same route. I had never associated my own species with the lower order of creatures in the matter of birth. I challenged Snooky with the stork story.

Snooky was up to the challenge. He told me in minute detail from beginning to end the graphic facts of human reproduction. I was dumbfounded. Then exhilarated. I was convinced that Snooky was telling the truth. I had made a glorious discovery. I was cautious, however. It contradicted the truth as my mother had described it. I sensed that the matter was not one to be discussed around adults or my sisters. The first chance I got to unfold my great discovery did not come until the following Sunday.

There were half a dozen children in my Sunday school class, known as Jesus' Little Sunbeams. We sat in small red chairs in a semicircle around our teacher, Miss Gertrude Holder, or "Miss Trudy" as she was addressed by one and all. Miss Trudy was what was in those days called an old maid. She was single and approaching middle age. She looked after her invalid father and worked as a secretary. Her devotion to her father was matched only by her devotion to our church and to the Little Sunbeams.

On this particular Sunday Miss Trudy announced that she had an exciting secret to disclose.

"Frank and Annie Lee Thomas are not here this Sunday," she said. "They have gone up to Oak Hill to stay with their grandparents. Sometime next week an old stork is going to fly down over South Austin and is going to circle and land on the Thomas house and leave a sweet little baby. Next Sunday Frank and Annie Lee will be back and tell us whether the stork brought them a little sister or a little brother. Now, isn't that exciting?"

We clapped and nodded dutifully. A moment later the Sunday school superintendent, Mr. Cappell, called Miss Trudy out of the classroom, which was actually a compartment formed by movable beaverboard partitions, about six feet high.

When she was out of the room, I leaned forward and explained to my fellow Sunbeams that Miss Trudy didn't know what she was talking about: Frank and Annie Lee's mother was going to have the baby. The stork part was nonsense. The Sunbeams were all ears in a second.

I was stage center and I made the most of it. I explained in a sure voice just how the baby came to be in Mrs. Thomas's stomach and exactly how it would make its appearance on the scene. I was no longer whispering but giving a robust report on the matter while the Sunbeams sat entranced, their jaws slack and eyes bugging.

I was in the process of taking questions from my audience when Miss Trudy charged into the room, her face a mask of white fury. She had been standing outside the compartment listening to my every word. She reached down, caught me by the left ear in a vise-like grip with one hand, and slapped me on the side of the head with the other.

I was too stunned by the sudden violence of her attack to feel anything but terror. Announcing I was not fit to remain in God's house, she hauled me out of class and deposited me on the back steps of the church, admonishing me to stay there while she went to report my sin to my mother, who was teaching a group of teenagers up at the front of the church.

Mixed in with the outrage that I felt as I sat snuffling on the church steps looking off across Newton Street was the realization that my crime, unpremeditated as it was, placed me outside the protective sympathy of family, church, and community. I remained under the cloud of that transgression for many days.

Before I had been restored to the good graces of my family, I was in trouble again. Snooky and the truth were once again the indirect causes.

Snooky and I were playing down on the creek near the lane that led only to the Bates's home. Brother Scott Cappell, our Sunday school superintendent, came down the lane in his yellow-wheeled buggy drawn by his sorrel mare. She was traveling at a brisk pace.

"I wonder why Brother Cappell is going up to your house," I said.

Snooky grinned. "He goin' to see my sister Letha Mae. He give her fifty cents to sweetheart with him."

He then described exactly what he meant by Brother Cappell's sweethearting with Letha Mae. It struck me as odd indeed since I had heard Brother Cappell speak sternly of "the need to keep darkies in their place." I had also heard my mother frequently speak of Brother Cappell's piety and virtue. When I told her what Snooky had related to me about Brother Cappell and Letha Mae sweethearting, my mother reacted as though Snooky and I were the sinners.

"Don't you ever repeat anything like that again, young man," she warned. "You stay away from that Snooky. Brother Cappell is one of the finest men in our church."

As often as I saw Brother Cappell thereafter, his horse and buggy tied in the cedar thicket near Snooky's house, I never brought up the matter with anyone.

But I learned a lesson about life: sometimes a simple truth can get you into a sight more trouble than a piece of obvious fiction. It is much safer to use deception and evasion than it is to confront the truth head-on.

It was this situation that led to an amazing discovery when I was about nine years old. One day my mother told me she was planning to invite the ladies of her missionary society over, and directed me to clean up the yard that day, including the chicken pen. It so happened I had been expecting company that day. Several friends were coming up to play cowboys and Indians. I knew without protesting, however, that Mama's church ladies took precedence, so I went to work. In shooing the hens out of the henhouse, I caught up one, holding her feet with one hand. I grasped her neck with the other and squeezed her windpipe. When I released the squeeze on her neck she let out a squawk as she gasped for breath. When I closed my hand on her neck, she was silenced.

A wondrous thought occurred to me that caused me to tingle all over. I slipped back to the kitchen window with the hen under my arm and, situating myself under the sill, said in my best imitation of a lady's voice, "The Women's Missionary Society will please come to order. Sister Allen, will you please call the roll."

Then in the creaky voice of Sister Allen I intoned: "Sis-ter Talley?" and released the hen's neck, at which she let out a squawk. I said, "Sis-ter Brodie?" "Cwa-a-a-k." "Sis-ter Forbis?" "Cwa-a-a-k." Alternately squeezing and releasing the hen's neck, I went through the roll call of all the members of my mother's church group.

I expected my mother, who did not allow her cherished institutions to be mocked, to come sailing out the kitchen door after me. I sat quiet and still, ready to feign innocence and explain I was only trying my best to keep the hen quiet but that my hand had slipped off her neck. To my delight, my sisters were in a near-hysterical state of laughter in the kitchen. My mother, trying without success to keep laughter out of her own voice, ordered: "Now you get yourself and that hen back out to the henhouse and get busy, young man, or I will make you wish you had."

It was at that time I began to understand a wondrous fact about humor. If I could gild my resentments and angers with laughter, I could express my real feelings without fear of punishment.

In those days I came to live in two separate worlds with distinct boundaries. Both were encompassed in South Austin, a neighborhood containing the farms of people like my father, a successful lawyer, as well as the shacks and tents of the poor black and white families living "down on the creek."

One was the world of my mother and my sisters, the Methodist world of churchgoing, hardworking, homeowning respectability. This world minded its manners, observed the amenities, and never used swear words. I abided by this world's rules as best I could on those occasions when I found myself caught up in its doings with no way to escape.

The other world was that of Snookie Bates: the poor blacks and the poor whites of South Austin who eked out a living chopping cedar, making charcoal, and doing menial work; a world that did not involve churchgoing and observing social amenities; a world outside the bounds of respectability.

A special friend of mine, Mr. John Brodie, lived in this latter world, although he was not one of its poor. He owned a farm that adjoined our place. He viewed the world of respectability with good-humored scorn, but he treated me with respect and affectionate kindness and always spoke to me as an equal. Not many adults treated ten-year-old boys that way in those days. And none that I knew shared his generous store of colorful, uninhibited ribald speech as well as his unorthodox views on South Austin society as freely as Mr. Brodie did. He confided to me quite frequently that considerable numbers of our respectable churchgoing neighbors were nothing more than "highly constipated fakers."

Riding along in his wagon one afternoon, I asked him what the word *feces* meant. I had heard it used that morning. He was ready with an answer.

"*Feces* is what church folks say when they mean *shit*."

One hot summer day I was riding with Mr. Brodie and one of his neighbors out near the municipal golf course in Austin. A tire went flat. While the neighbor and I changed it, Mr. Brodie stood watching some golfers on the fairway across the fence from us. Golf knickers were in vogue back in those days, and a number of the players were wearing them.

After watching the golfers for an interval, Mr. Brodie asked, "Johnny, what the hell are those fellers doing over there?"

"That's golf, Mr. Brodie," I replied. "They are playing golf."

"Playing golf!" he exploded. "By God, no wonder the world is coming apart! Full-grown men, rigged out in knee pants, wandering around in the broiling sun, chasing a ball the size of a pullet egg, and calling it a game!"

After we had changed the tire and were pulling away, Mr. Brodie nudged me in the ribs and commented, "Johnny, I bet you that ever' one of them golf fellers squats to pee." He never explained why he thought golf was an effeminate game.

Mr. Brodie's love for robust language was matched by another friend of mine, Boots Corder, who was something of a virtuoso in that department. Boots could swear prodigiously, throw a rock as far as a grown man could, and chew tobacco like one. He could go to school or stay home just as he pleased. I counted him one of the most fortunate people I ever met. Just one streak of his spectacular profanity within my mother's hearing was more than enough to mark him persona non grata around our house. This ban only drove our friendship underground. We spent hours on spring afternoons and during weekends roaming the woods, crawfishing in the creek, and practicing our profanity.

While my family lived in a great house with spacious verandas on a forty-acre farm, down on the creek a half a mile away a number of itinerant families—including the Corders—existed in ragged tents and unheated lean-to shacks. The poor were unmistakably poor. They lived in grim poverty, surviving by selling charcoal and wood and doing whatever odd jobs came along. Some of the families had only one or two cooking utensils. Most often their meal was cornmeal mush with bacon grease. When it was served up, all the children stood around a big trough or container and passed a spoon. Few of them had more than one garment. They slept in the same clothes they wore all day. The children of these families carried about them the faint odor of stale urine.

The world of respectability had Easter-egg hunts, Christmas trees, and Sunday school picnics. The other world seldom knew except by rumor that a holiday had arrived.

One Christmas Day, one of my playmates came running up to our house to report the wondrous Christmas his family was experiencing that year. His father had gone into town, where Santa Claus had given him a gift for each of his seven children. Rufus held up an orange.

I had seen hundreds of oranges. I said, "Shucks, Rufus, that ain't nothing but an orange. That ain't no real Christmas present." As soon as the words were out of my mouth I knew I had blundered. Rufus stared at me in hurt and puzzlement.

"It's the onliest orange I ever had," he said softly.

Neither my sisters nor my Sunday school friends shared my attachment to the other world, black or white. They especially took exception to my mimicking their speech and relating stories about the black folk.

My method, as I developed it to trap my critics into hearing what I had to say, was to set my listeners to laughing with funny anecdotes about my poor and black friends. I would mimic Aunt Harriet Williams explaining to me why she did not value a quarter that was worn smooth: "Why, it ain't no good. That old slickry quarter done wore out. You cain't even see the hawk on it no more."

Once my listeners were laughing and asking for more I would slip in an account of a black family who had to stay in bed under the covers in the bitter winter; they had neither clothes to fend off the cold nor wood to build a fire in their stove.

My notion of first-rate entertainment was my father's method of trying a lawsuit down at the Travis County Courthouse. His use of the idiom of rural Texas, his mastery of mimicry and satire, won him a sizable following in any courtroom where he appeared.

He would convert the courtroom into a stage, with the jury, the spectators, and the judge all a part of his audience. He would mimic the opposing attorney and any hostile witnesses. The jurors would grin broadly and sometimes burst into laughter. The judge would rap for order, trying without success to suppress his own laughter. Daddy would then go through a mock display of apologizing to the court and to his opposing attorney, and refrain briefly from his performance. But within a matter of minutes he was at it again.

In one case, Daddy came up against an arrogant opponent we'll call Lawyer Hominy, who had flowing white hair and grand airs. Daddy knew that Lawyer Hominy's weakness was his vanity.

"If a client is represented by a pompous jackass," he said to the jury, gesturing ever so slightly at the other table.

Mr. Hominy popped out of his seat, red-faced and angry. "Your honor, Mr. Faulk is obviously referring to me as a pompous jackass. I ask the Court to direct him to refrain from personal references to me."

The judge, hand shielding his smile, directed Daddy to refrain from any more personal references to Hominy.

Daddy, feigning distress and bewilderment, replied, "I hope Mr. Hominy will accept my apologies. I had no idea he would regard any mention of a pompous jackass in a hypothetical instance as applying to him personally."

Much of my father's language and wisdom came from his odd mixture of egalitarian philosopher, biblical scholar, lawyer, and teacher. Although he was an agnostic, he was a pillar of the Methodist Church and taught adult Bible class.

"Jesus was a philosopher, Johnny," he was fond of saying. "His truth had a way of taking the bark off a tree, and it hasn't grown back since."

He had been raised in poverty as a sharecropper, and he never forgot it. Through a stroke of good fortune, he had learned to read and write, had worked his way through the University of Texas, and had become a successful lawyer.

He believed that because he had made it, it was necessary for him to see that others had the chance. My father was convinced of the perfectibility of man. The endless array of relatives, both his and my mother's, who came to stay at our home and receive his lectures on the importance of education and hard work were testimonies to his belief in perfectibility, rather than a confidence in his success at getting them to that state.

My father believed that James Madison's First Amendment was the linchpin of our liberties. He pronounced this truth to all who would listen, or who paused long enough in his vicinity to receive the message, whether they wanted to or not. He believed that mankind's perfectibility required his constant attention and goading.

If imitation is the sincerest form of flattery, I flattered my father constantly. My concern for social justice was inspired by him. As I went into my teens, I began to use mimicry and satire to make social comment in the style he had set.

By the time I was sixteen, I had begun to enjoy a degree of local fame for my ear for rural Texas dialect and black folk idiom. Like Daddy, I used my skill as a mimic sometimes for idle fun, sometimes for another purpose.

One day my friend Jack Burnet and I were down at Chum's Feed Store. Mr. Max Sherman, a well-to-do white insurance man, had come into the store to buy chicken feed. He said something to a teenage black delivery boy, who was standing inside the store.

Apparently the boy gave him an insolent reply, for suddenly Mr. Sherman flew into a rage, knocked the boy to the floor, and began to kick him, while muttering between clenched teeth, "Don't you ever speak to a white man like that, nigger. Or I'll knock that woolly head off your shoulders."

The boy, bruised and dazed, lay shielding his face from the kicks. The brutality of the attack sickened me.

Mr. Sherman calmly went to the faucet, washed his hands, and called over his shoulder to the groaning boy, "Now you get up and get out of here."

Shaken and angry when we got home, Jack and I discussed the injustice of the savage attack as we sat on the front porch. I was suddenly inspired. Looking up Max Sherman's telephone number in the phone book, I dialed slowly. I took on the voice of an indignant black woman and asked for Mr. Max Sherman.

I heard Sherman's son call, "Some nigger gal wants you, Dad." When he answered, I said, "You old yellow-bellied egg-sucking Max Sherman."

"Who—who are you?" he stammered.

"You going to find out who I is when my husband come down there and kick your white butt up and down South Congress Avenue. You ain't nothing but a yellow-bellied coward. You might pick on little colored boys, but you won't stand up to no real colored man. You too yellow."

Sherman sounded like a mad bull as he roared, "By God, you just let him come. Send him up here. Tell me where you are, and I'll come down there. Who are you—I dare you to give me your name."

He had taken the bait. He was mine to play with. I had discovered the Achilles heel of bigotry. From now on, I could punish him at leisure, and sit down while I did it. Safely. Jack was awed with my virtuoso performance as I tormented Mr. Sherman with stinging insults for a quarter of an hour.

"You really fooled that old rascal," Jack beamed.

Jack did not know what I did. I was rejoicing in the agony I caused Sherman, not in just fooling him.

I was beginning to understand what Daddy meant when he said that segregation was a disease that punished the perpetrator as cruelly as the victim. I was also learning that humor could be manipulated like a scalpel.

In the years that followed, I polished my scalpel. One day at dinner my mother spoke in a warm, approving tone of old Mr. Tucker, a devoted member of our church who gave generously toward its upkeep. I knew him to be a conscienceless taskmaster to the black sharecroppers on his bottomland farm, whom he worked hard and paid little. I agreed that Brother Tucker was indeed filled with the spirit of Jesus.

"He was telling me just last week how considerate and kind he is with his hired hands," I said with all seriousness. "He said when he had to give one of his niggers a whipping, he always tried to remember the nigger's feelings."

" 'I don't just call him out in front of his wife and children and give him a whupping,' " I mimicked Brother Tucker's voice. " 'That would be wrong. That would break his spirit. I drive him down in the woods out of sight and whup him there. Let me tell you, my niggers appreciate my thoughtfulness.' "

By the time I got to the University of Texas, I had become something of an entertainer. I enjoyed regaling audiences with my stories and

imitations of blacks, poor whites, bigots and the many characters
I met or invented. However, it was not until I got into the class
taught by Mr. J. Frank Dobie at the university that I came to truly
value the rich color and imagery of the native material I had found.

Mr. Dobie was a professor of English literature who had won
a national reputation as a folklorist and collector of Mexican folk
legends.

I was an indifferent student, content with mediocre grades. But
Mr. Dobie changed that. He became enthralled with the characters
I mimicked and delighted in my stories. He gave my material credit
for a worth I had long suspected. Mr. Dobie got me to join the Texas
Folklore Society, which he and his friend John A. Lomax, the pioneer
of American folklore, had helped found. He introduced me to Alan
Lomax, John A.'s son, also an experienced folklorist who was about
my age. Alan taught me what folklore was really all about.

Mr. Dobie's class, "Life and Literature of the Southwest," was filled
to overflowing with students who came under his spell. Although
he was a brilliant scholar, he eschewed the role of academician.

Mr. Dobie maintained several dozen head of cattle on his ranch
outside Austin. He kept a good cow horse there so he could work
his cattle himself. He had been a working cowboy most of his life.
One afternoon, he arrived for an English faculty meeting, coming
directly from his ranch in muddy boots and work clothes. As several
senior professors argued a purely academic point of trivial importance, Dobie leaned towards me, his snowy white hair hanging over
his ruddy countenance, and mumbled, "Here go the pee-dogies
[pedagogues], Johnny, moving dry bones from one graveyard to
another."

Instead of pursuing minute academic concerns, he gloried in the
earthy folk story and poetry of Texas. He championed the creativity
of our local bards and tale-spinners. Mr. Dobie claimed that the
Texas mockingbird sounded just as sweet as the British poets'
nightingales and larks. He said that lyric poetry was beautiful
wherever it was created.

To illustrate his point, he would stride up and down, declaiming
a poem by Lord Byron:

> The Isles of Greece, the Isles of Greece,
> Where burning Sappho loved and sung,
> Where talk is made of war and peace,
> Where Phoebus rose and Delos sprung.
> Eternal summer gilds them yet
> Though all except their sun has set.

Mr. Dobie would rhapsodize over Byron's lyrical talent. "What melodic verse, what lyrical poetry," he would proclaim. Then he would break into a rousing cowboy song:

> Sam Bass was born in Indiana, it was his native home;
> And at the age of seventeen young Sam began to roam;
> He first came to Texas, a cowboy to be,
> A kinder-hearted fellow you'll seldom ever see.
>
> Young Sam he dealt in race stock, one called the Denton mare;
> He matched her at scrub races and carried her to the fair;
> Sam always coined the money and spent it very free,
> He always drank good whiskey, wherever he might be.

Then Mr. Dobie would grin like Santa Claus coming out of the chimney and ask the class: "Which has the greatest measure of poetry and spirit-lifting imagery in it? I say they are on a par!"

Under Mr. Dobie's influence, I went searching for folklore throughout rural Texas. He became impressed with the sermons of rural black preachers I had collected, and urged me to do my master's thesis on them. Like Dobie's favorite Texas poetry, these sermons followed an epic pattern, filled with rich folk imagery.

During World War II, in the merchant marine, in the American Red Cross Field Service, and as a G.I., I honed my skills at telling folk anecdotes. My willingness to perform with the characters I had developed and polished kept me in something like a chronic state of entertaining.

Several days after I was discharged from the army in April 1946, I went up to New York to go on CBS Radio as a folk humorist and storyteller. My principal stock-in-trade on the air was relating tales and anecdotes about folk characters in Texas, most of them my neighbors and relatives.

It was my belief that from the earliest days of this republic, American humor has had a unique flavor, an egalitarian quality that sets it apart from the laughter of other societies.

Ours was the first society dedicated to the proposition that the people were the masters and the government was the servant, a society in which the granting of titles and privileges was forever banned. It was the first government established that contained an absolute guarantee that the people could think about, speak about, and laugh at the most powerful forces in the land without fear of punishment.

Humor was used from the very start in this country to puncture pomposity and ridicule pretentiousness. During the nineteenth century Josh Billings, Bill Nye, and others brought humor to something of an art. Mark Twain made it a high art. His observations such as, "There is only one criminal class in the United States — the United States Congress," brought laughter around the country a hundred years ago. They still do.

Most of the humor I have heard and cherished from my childhood forward derives from this egalitarian origin. This happy practice of using humor for social and political comment has an irresistible appeal to me.

II
The Scent of Magnolias

II

When John Henry Faulk set out on a career in radio in the 1940s, his reputation was based on his stories of southern life and the regional speech of his native Texas. Their enduring quality is such that after forty years, audiences still call for Faulk's explanation for why we have Republicans in the United States today, a piece enjoyed by Democrats and Republicans alike.

Not all of Faulk's stories were lighthearted. Also typical of his themes is "A Glorious Fourth," a tale of unthinking racial brutality told by a casual observer who nevertheless cuts directly to the bone and nerve of American life.

The Care and Feeding of Republicans

About this early Faulk classic, John Henry states: "In the early 1940s, when I was teaching English at the University of Texas, I was asked to entertain at a big dinner given in honor of Mr. George Dealey, publisher of the Dallas Morning News. The editorial policy of the News was so strongly anti-Roosevelt and pro-Republican that I decided to do a plea for the preservation of Republicans on reservations, by way of having a bit of sport at Mr. Healey's expense. I used a genial Texas character I had named Cousin Claude to present the case for The Care and Feeding of Republicans. It should be recalled that in 1941, Roosevelt had soundly trounced the Republicans three times, and it did seem as though the Republicans would never make a comeback."

COUSIN CLAUDE: Folks, I want everybody in this audience that has ever seen an honest-to-God live Republikin to hold up his hand.

(After a pause:) Just like I thought. Not a single one of you. You know why none of you ever seen a live one? Because they have all but disappeared.

Actually, most people in Texas is plumb Republikin ignernt. Yessir, Republikin ignernt. Wouldn't know a Republikin if they met it standing in the middle of the road.

Most Texans is plumb confused on the subject. Take ol' man Mosteller. He's a good man, a Baptist deacon, and wouldn't lie if you paid him to. But he's confused. Told me last week that sure, he knowed what a Republikin is. He's caught many a one, running 'em with his dogs. They got a shell on and mostly come out at night to root around ol' dead stumps.

See what I mean? Old Man Mosteller has got Republikins confused with armadillos. In other words, he's Republikin ignernt.

I ain't being critical when I say that I used to be ignernt myself about Republikins. I was plumb growed 'fore I ever seen one! Never will forgit. I was sitting out on the back porch reading the *Dallas Morning News.* I seen a picture in the paper and it said, "Thomas E. Dewey." Then next to that was the word "Republican."

Well, the truth come to me in a blinding flash, and I called Mama. I said, "Mama, come here quick. Did you ever see a Republikin?"

She said, "No, I ain't."

I says, "Wish you'd look at *that!*"

She stares at the picture and says, "Lord have mercy! Is that one?"

I says, "Shore is!"

She says, "Why hit's got clothes on, ain't it!"

There you are. Me and Mama was both Republikin ignernt. Just like you folks and everybody else in Texas.

You know why?

'Cause we've gone and left open season on Republikins in Texas for so long, we done thinned 'em out to nothing.

But it ain't that way everywhere. My Cousin Ernie took a load of melons up to a place called Westchester County in New York. He says he found a whole pack of Republikins up there. Great big ol' fat gentle things. So tame you could walk right up to them. And you know why? They are protected by law up there, that's why.

Ernie says they ain't exactly numerous, but they are managing to hold on.

Now Ernie puts it like this:

What would of happened to the buffalo in America if public-spirited citizens hadn't took steps to preserve them? They'd been wiped out, that's what. Well, me and Ernie maintains that the Republikin is just as much a part of our historic past in America as the buffalo is.

It's our patriotic duty to preserve them!

You might say, "Well, you so enthusiastic over having people look at Republikins, why don't you stuff a pair like they do up in Washington and set 'em down there on the Courthouse Square where everybody can go look at 'em?"

Let me tell you something 'bout that! Them ain't stuffed ones in Washington. They jest seem that way. They're real honest-to-God live Republikins. I maintain Texas is entitled to some, too!

So here's what I'm proposin'
Settin' up a reservation in one of our state parks
Fix it up real natural
And old-timey lookin'—
Get a hold of a small drove of Republikins—

Put them out there—
Then leave them to theirselves.
Don't leave any clocks or calendars around.
Republikins don't like to know what century
They're living in
Let alone what year it is.

Oh yes, and be sure to fix it up
So they can't hurt theirselves.
Republikins is more interested in where
They come *from*
Than where they're goin' *to*.
This means they're always lookin' backwards.
It causes them to run into things.

Also, put somebody in to supervise 'em
That understands Republikin feelin's.
You don't want somebody who likes
To tease Republikins—
Somebody that will yell "Roosevelt"
Or "New Deal" in their presence.

That'll cause a Republikin to
Swell up and sulk—
Shut both eyes and tremble.
He won't take nourishment for a week
When he's in one of them pouts.

No, what you want is somebody in charge
That understands and sympathizes with Republikins,
That will be gentle and kind with them.

After all, our whole purpose is to
Preserve the Republikin.
Preserve this historic memento
Of Yesterday in America!
Symbol of the Past!
The Republikin Party!

A Glorious Fourth

Me and Earl was invited over to Turk and Eller's place for the Fourth
of July. Eller's my sister. Her and her husband Turk sort of took
me over after Mama died. They never liked Earl much. They blamed
him for getting me to drop out of high school and move in with
him at his rooming house. But they was wrong. Earl never had to
get me to do it. I was tired of being broke all the time and never
gittin' to go nowhere. So when Earl told me I could share them two
rooms with him, I jumped at the chance. Then, 'course, he got me
a job there at the filling station, working nights. That made it 'bout
perfect.

Turk and Eller never hold nothing against a person long. So when
she stopped by the filling station to invite me over to eat with them
on the Fourth, she told me to bring Earl, too.

Turk got us into a game of horseshoes before we got good set
down. He beat both of us about five straight games. Earl said, "Hell,
Turk, you too good. Let's set up there on the porch where there's
some shade. Play dominoes. Too damn hot out here in the sun."

Turk shook his head. "I'm in that mill all day ever' day. I git a
chance to git out in the air, I ain't going to pass it up." He just went
on pitching horseshoes at the posts, like he was playing somebody.
Me and Earl went up and sat down in the porch swing.

The sun was really pouring it on. You could see the heat waves
shimmerin' along the top of the fence. Everything in the neighborhood was takin' it easy. The only sounds you could hear, besides
Turk a-gittin' ringers, was Ella fixin' dinner in the kitchen and a
couple of hens cacklin' over in Mrs. Musset's barn. Even the locusts
had stopped singing out. There wern't enough breeze to stir the long
moss on the oak trees over there at the Baptist Church.

We heard a car coming up the road from towards the mill. Earl,
he knows cars. He always says he's goin' to be a mechanic one of
these days. He cocked his ear. "Bet you four bits that's Raymond

Cannon's Chevy. I kin tell by the way the engine's missin' out." Sure enough, in a minute ol' Raymond come a-steaming around the bend in that '29 Chevy of his. He pulled up at the gate. Turk called, "Howdy Ray. Git out and come in. I was just a-hopin' that somebody would come along and play me a game of horseshoes. Alvin and Earl's skeered."

Raymond jumped out of his car. "Horseshoes, hell. Ain't you heard? Nigger stabbed Deppity Sheriff Ross this morning down at Patton's Corners. Sheriff Hicks wants us all up at the Courthouse right away. Wants us to help round up that nigger. Come on. Bring your guns if you got 12 gauges. Sheriff's got buckshot."

Me and Earl was done up and ready. Turk just stood there holding the horseshoes. He don't hurry about nothin' like that.

Raymond asked if he had a drink in the house. Turk shook his head. "We don't keep none, Ray. Reckin the boys and me better not go along. Eller's fixin' a big dinner for us. Been cookin' all morning. She wouldn't want us runnin' off." Turk never did have no appetite for gitting mixed up in trouble.

Raymond spit, "Why, goddam, Turk, you ain't going to let a bad nigger run loose, are you? Sheriff ain't going to like it if you don't come. He said get every white man I could find. Hit ain't goin' to take us long to search Cow Flats. Sheriff says that's where the nigger's hidin'." Cow Flats is the colored section of town. I don't know how it got that name. But it's always been called Cow Flats.

Turk just stood there shaking his head no. "They don't need us, Raymond. That's business for police. That boy'll probably give hisself up to the law."

Me and Earl was anxious. Earl started in the house. "I'll tell Eller that we got business to do—she kin hold off dinner awhile." Raymond was waiting. He called, "Tell her you'll be back in a couple of hours. Hellfire, Turk. This here's the Fourth of July. Don't you want to celebrate the Fourth?" Turk shook his head. "Not that way, I don't."

I went in the kitchen. Earl was funnin' Ella, tellin' her we had to go save the country. Ella didn't like our going off. She hadn't started fryin' the chicken, but she said, "Y'all ain't got no business runnin' off like this. I been over this hot cook stove all mornin'. My head's jest splittin' and my throat's hurtin' right where Mama's hurt." Ella's always skeered she's got cancer of the throat like Mama had.

Earl kept on a jollyin' her, "Aw, Eller, ain't you heared of the Glorious Fourth? Folks s'pose' to celebrate. Me and Alvin will clean up everythin' after dinner, I swear." Earl can talk a woman into anything. Ella was pouting, but she give in. "Well, if y'all ain't back in two hours, everythin' is goin' to be cold." We got Turk's shotgun out of the closet and went out in the front yard. Turk said he reckoned if we was goin' he had better go along, too. We all climbed into Raymond's car and took off.

On the way up to the courthouse, Raymond told us what had happened at Patton's Corners. He said Deputy Ross had come down there to arrest some colored crapshooters, and one of the boys had run up and stabbed him in the back. The deputy went down and the boy run.

It bein' a holiday, most of the men around Pineville was off work. There must of been twenty fellows standing and squattin' around in the shade. Most of them had shotguns or rifles. Sheriff Hicks was standin' under one of them big magnolia trees near the courthouse steps. I could tell he was madder'n all git-out. He was stomping around and he was whupping the leaves off of the low branches of the tree with his cane. Earl nudged me. "Ol' High Sheriff's mad, all right. Look at him." Raymond peeled back his lips in that sideways grin of his. "He's got a right to be mad! Niggers out stabbin' his deputies all the time."

Earl laughed, "Yeah, but he better not let Miss Elsie Patton ketch him tearin' up that magnolier tree that-away. She'll make him fergit all about his depitties and cuttin' niggers." I said, "That's right. Papa used to say that Elsie Patton counted every leaf on them trees. Thought more of them than she did of human beings." Miss Elsie Patton is a old maid that sort of runs the town. Her folks used to own about everything in these parts. She planted them magnolia trees long before I was born. Named one "Mother" and the other one "Father." Reckin them's the only trees with names in Texas.

Sheriff Hicks called us all together. He can sure look mean when he wants to. He started out in that bullfrog voice of his. "Boys, you all know what happened. I just want to say that my deputy, Ross, might die. Doctor's still working on him. But I ain't goin' to have no nigger cutting up my boys. We got word that that boy that done the cuttin' is hiding out there in Cow Flats. I'm deputizing all of you, till we bring him in. I want Raymond Cannon to take half of you and go up to the north end of Cow Flats. I want Dick Scantling to take the rest of you down to the south end. I want you to check every shack and shed and corncrib out there. I don't want no showin' off and hell raisin'. I want that boy." He passed out buckshot to them with shotguns.

A bunch of us piled into Ray's car with four or five hanging on the running boards. I'd done got so worked up that I even forgot how hot it was. We was all laughin' and jokin' like we was on our way to a Sunday school picnic.

Except Turk. He didn't say a word. Just set there between me and Raymond in the front seat and looked straight ahead. Bud Archer was following along behind us with some fellows in his Ford coup. It's a '28, but he's always hurrahing Raymond about his Ford, old as it is, being better than Raymond's Chevy. He would keep honkin' and pullin' up behind Raymond like he was tryin' to pass us. Raymond was cussin' mad. He don't like for nobody to crowd him like that.

We stopped by Wendy's store. It sits right at the north end of the road that runs up through Cow Flats. I call it a road. Some folks call it a street, but it ain't nothing but a sandy lane, really. The colored folks' houses, or shacks, are scattered along each side for about a half mile. When we got out of the cars, we could see the people sittin' on their front porches and kids playin' 'round in the yards. They was most of them off for the day, even if it wasn't their Fourth. When they seen us startin' down the road with guns, they started fading into their houses in a hurry, calling to the kids to git in, too.

By the time we started into the first shack, you couldn't see a colored person stirrin' nowheres. They are skittish that way. I couldn't help feelin' kind of important.

When we would come up to a place, we'd have to go in. We couldn't get them out. Raymond would cuss and yell, "Open her up, or we'll kick the goddam door in." And he'd hurl off and kick the door durn near off the hinges. Or he would threaten to just start shootin' into the house.

Most of the shacks didn't have but two or three rooms, so it didn't take long to search them. The colored folks would back up in a corner and wall their eyes. In a couple of places they pretended that they were sick, and laid in bed with the covers over them. Raymond would jerk the quilts off and they would just lay there, with all their clothes on.

In one shack there was a old woman and her three kids. One was a girl about sixteen, I reckon. She was light brown, and a pretty good looker for a colored girl. She and the old lady and the other two kids was pushed up agin the wall, plumb wide-eyed scaired. Raymond walked over to her and winked, "Gal, you shore you ain't hiding that boy up under your dress?" She shook her head, and looked like she didn't understand. "She deef," the old woman sort of stuttered out. Raymond grinned and motioned for her to pull up her dress.

Turk hadn't said nothin' since we had left home. He looked right at Raymond, "Come on, Ray, that ain't what we come here for. Let's git out of here! Right now!"

We got out in a hurry. Raymond come out. He was peeved at Turk, but he tried to joke it off, "Hellfar, Turk, you ain't got no sense of humor. I wasn't goin' to hurt that girl." Turk didn't say nothin', but I knowed he wasn't enjoyin' the business.

We would see colored people tryin' to sneak out the back of their shacks and run for the woods. Raymond would yell, "Stop where you're at or I'll shoot." They would stop. One old man, called Pegleg on account of he had a peg leg, was hobblin' out of his place when we came around the corner of his shack. Raymond hollered and the old man throwed both hands up in the air. He's kind of touched in the head. Raymond said, "Peg, goddammit, what do you mean by tryin' to sneak off? How in the hell you think you goin' to git away on that peg leg?" The old fellow didn't look 'round. Just kept his hands up. Raymond winked at us, and said, "You know better 'n to sneak off from the law. I ought to kill you where you stand, you old devil. But I'm goin' to give you a chance. If you can make it to them bushes before I count ten, I won't shoot you. Now git." It was near fifty yards to the woods, but old Pegleg took off like a cripple turkey. Raymond let him git about half way, then he pointed his gun straight up in the air and shot. Pegleg thought he was killed for sure. He fell on the ground headfirst and just laid there.

I started to laugh but looked at Turk and decided not to. Raymond called out, "You'll have to git somebody else to bury you, Peg. We're in a hurry." And we started to the next shack. Peg hadn't started gettin' up when I looked back.

We could see Buck Scantling and his bunch down at the far end. They was goin' in and out of houses. Raymond started hurryin' us up. I didn't know why at first. I asked Earl why Raymond was gittin' such a move on. He nodded his head towards a house a little ways down the road. "Ray wants to git to Arthur Franklin's place before Buck gits there. He's been layin' for old Franklin a long time." Then I knew.

Arthur Franklin is the colored school superintendent. He ain't exactly uppity, but he sort of give hisself airs sometimes. Him and his wife come here about five years ago when the county commissioners decided to put in a superintendent for the colored schools. He called hisself Professor Franklin. Drives a durn good car, too. 1935 Buick. He keeps it just as shiny as the day he got it. He used to drive into Raymond's filling station with his wife and just sit there, waiting for Raymond to take care of him. Old Raymond did it a couple of times, but one time he told Raymond to check his tires and put water in the radiator. That done it. Raymond backed off and give him a cussin' and told him he didn't want his business.

There was a white picket fence around Franklin's yard and all sorts of flowers planted. The house was new-lookin' white and yellow. If it hadn't been in Cow Flats, you would never know colored people lived there. Raymond told a couple of the boys to go around in back in case Franklin tried to run. Turk stopped in the road. He looked at Raymond hard. "Ray, you know that Franklin wouldn't hide nobody in his place." Raymond grinned and kicked the gate open. He motioned for us to go in. He said, "You heered what the sheriff said, Turk. Search ever' place. That's what I aim to do. Come on."

Me and Earl was sort of anxious to git into Franklin's house. We had heard all sorts of tales about how fine it was inside. Folks said he had 'lectric iceboxes, big pianos, and all sorts of stuff in there.

We walked up on the porch and Raymond banged on the door with the butt of his gun. Franklin opened it and we could tell that he had been expectin' us. But he didn't make a move to let us in. Just stood there. He was scared. But he didn't move. Raymond said, "We're here in the name of the law. Sheriff ordered us to search this house." Franklin didn't move and his face didn't change. He said polite-like, "You're welcome to search my home. Do you have a search warrant?" That stopped Raymond flat. We hadn't even thought of no search warrant. Nobody else had asked us for one. Raymond's face was twisted and his teeth was showin'. He turned plumb red in the face. He said, sort of lame-like, "We're all deputized. We don't need no warrant. We're here under orders from Sheriff Hicks." Franklin still didn't move. He nodded, "This is a private home. It's illegal to enter this house without a search warrant." Turk had come up. He said, "He's right Ray. We ain't got no right in his house without no search warrant. We better get one before we make trouble." Just for a minute Franklin looked at Turk, nodding. Raymond's face was harder 'n a snake's. All the sudden he grunted, "By God, here's our warrant," and he brung the butt of his gun up under Franklin's chin. It made a crunching pop, Franklin's head snapped back and his glasses flew off. He fell like a sack of cow feed. His wife had been standin' a little behind him. She let out a scream and jumped at Raymond. He let her have it across the head with the barrel of his gun and down she went, out cold. Raymond stepped over them and called, "All right, boys, search the house. And search it good." We poured in after him. It was a clean place, but nothin' special. We didn't see no 'lectric icebox, but they did have a piano and a lot of Sears Roebuck furniture, that overstuffed kind. We knew we wasn't going to find that boy there. But we acted like we was looking. Old Raymond was havin' hisself a time. He was pullin' down pictures and turnin' over furniture and tearin' up the bed. "Never kin tell where that boy might hide," he said. After a little he called to us, "Ain't here, boys. Let's get goin'."

As we was goin' out, we stopped to look at Franklin and his wife. He was sitting up, holdin' his head, still dazed. She was layin' where she fell, moanin' and cryin'. One of the fellows asked Raymond, "Reckon they need some help, Ray?"

Raymond kept walkin', "Hell, no. They ain't hurt bad. Cain't hurt no nigger hittin' him in the head. Got to hit 'em on the heel to kill 'em. That's where their brains is." We all walked out into the road. Turk hadn't gone in the house. He was waitin' for us out there. We seen Sheriff Hicks comin' up the road in his Ford. He called out to us, "We got him, boys. He give hisself up at the courthouse. Come on down to my office. Got sodywater for the boys and something stronger for the men." A couple of fellows rode back with him and the rest of us started up through Cow Flats to our cars. The colored folks were still layin' low. Not a sign of them outside. The sun was right straight up over us, and it was blisterin' hot. As we walked past the shacks, Raymond would sing out, "You folks can come out. Celebration's over."

When we started back toward town in the car, Turk said, "You better take us on home, Ray. Eller'll be waiting dinner on us." Raymond grinned and looked at Turk out of the corner of his eye, "You don't need no dinner bad as you need a drink, Turk. Come on down and have jest one drink for the Fourth of July." Turk shook his head. "No, Ray, I don't want no drink for the Fourth of nothin'. Take us by home."

Me and Earl wanted to go down to the courthouse, but when Turk talks that way there ain't no arguing with him. Raymond joked about this and that, but he took us on home. We was gettin' out of the car and Raymond said, "Wish you would come along, boys. Turk, if you ain't keerful, folks are going to be saying you ain't got no patriotism." Turk never answered him. We went in and Ella was waitin' for us. Turk never ate much, said the heat must of got him. But me and Earl made up for him. We was hungry as starved dogs.

III
Sermons from the Field

III

Along with politics and racial problems, Faulk has been fascinated with the native speech of black people living in East Texas, who mainly worked as field hands on the river-bottom cotton plantations. To steep himself in the rhythms of their language, Faulk would attend religious services on Sunday evenings in the small rural churches back in the fields. Under the spell of powerful, often illiterate preachers, he would then go home to write up the sermons from his notes, using phonetic spelling to retain the rich speech patterns of the ministers.

This experience led to his writing his master's thesis at the University of Texas in 1940, titled "Ten Negro Sermons," the bibliography for which consisted of a single book: the Bible. Faulk's work in black folklore resulted in his receiving a grant from the Rosenwald Foundation to record black church music and black folklore for the Folk Archives at the Library of Congress. A duplicate of all the material was sent to the University of Texas folk archives at Faulk's request, so that it might be available for Texas scholars.

The two sermons included here are presented as he rendered them in his 1940 thesis. The first one, "How Much Does Ah Weigh?" was preached by the Reverend L. L. Laws at the Friendship Baptist Church in Littig, Texas, in 1939. The second sermon, "Ah Is de Way," was preached by the Reverend R. R. Reese in the Mt. Zion Baptist Church in Austin County, Texas, in 1940.

How Much Does Ah Weigh?

Well, dis trip's 'bout ovuh, an' de ol' chu'ch is still sailin' on. Amen. She's still trav'lin' de sea t'wawd salvation with huh load of saved souls. You know, dis ol' chu'ch ship might have some mighty rocky goin' sometimes, but she always pulls through. Amen. She gits in some mighty shalluh wawtuh, but she travels right on. We's been havin' a sho 'nough soul-savin' spurit-movin' time of hit fuh de pas' two weeks, an' hit seem like de ol' chu'ch ship's stronguh dan evuh. Amen.

Ah'm goin' to preach outten Danyul t'night. Ol' man Danyul have 'bout all the could do to keep de ol' chu'ch ship a-sailin', hisse'f, you know. He sholy did. Long 'bout ol' man Danyul's time, de ol' chu'ch ship was dippin' wawtuh fas' an' hit look like she was goin' to go plum' unduh jes' any day an' not come up agin. Amen.

But dey tells me ol' Danyul kep' a-fightin'. He nevuh give up. He didn't no quickuh git one knot untied, dan anothuh one run through his han's. But ol' man Danyul was a-prayin' chile, chu'ch, an' he nevuh give up. Dey might throw all his frien's in a fahry fuhness, an' dey might throw him in de lion's den, but Danyul went right on suhvin' his Lawd. An' he tol' dem ol' kaings dat dey bettuh watch how dey pranked with de Lawd, or dey was jes' liable to grab holt of somethin' dat dey couldn't tuhn loose. Yes, he did. Amen. Ol' man Danyul tol' dem kaings dat de Lawd done weigh 'em on his scales an' foun' 'em too light. Amen.

Ah'm goin' to ax a question with mah tex' t'night. Ah'm goin' to ax mahse'f, "How much does Ah weigh?" Ah wants evuhbody out dere to ax deyse'fs, "How much does Ah weigh?" Amen. Iffen we is Christians, we all wants to know how much we goin' to weigh out on jedgement day. Amen.

We always wants to know how much do things weigh, don't we? When we goes in town to de sto' an' buys us some cawnmeal or some sugah, we axes de man how much do hit weigh, don't we? We jes' pays de man fuh as much as hit weigh. Yes, we do. We likes to know how much cotton we picked, so we weighs hit. An' we gits paid fuh jes' as much as hit weighs an' no mo'. Dat's right. We don't git paid fuh what we think hit weigh. We gits paid fuh what de scales say hit weigh. Well, amen. We'd think de boss man done gone crazy iffen he stawted payin' us fuh whut we tol' 'im dat we thought de cotton weigh. Co'se we would.

So, hit's de same way with de Lawd. He got hisse'f some scales up dere an' he weigh out de amount of Christian dat dey is in evuh las' soul he take into glory. Amen. You might kin fool some folks 'bout how much Christian you got in you, but you cain't fool de Lawd. He got scales dat'll ketch evuh sin you has did. He sholy has. How much does Ah weigh? Amen. Ah wants de chu'ch to ax hitse'f, "How much does Ah weigh?"

Well, dey tells me dat ol' man Bushazzah was havin' a feas'. Yes, he was. He had all de big folks in de lan' dere. Amen. Dey was celebratin' jes' big as you please. Dey was singin' an' dancin' an' havin' a real to-do. Oh, yes dey was. Dey was sinnin' an' showin' off, an' not payin' no min' to nobody in de wul. Dey was laughin' at de chu'ch folks an' fuhgittin' dey're Gawd. Oh, yes dey was. Dey was havin' deyse'fs a sho 'nough feas'. An' ol' Bushazzah was de bellweathuh of de whole show. He was havin' a feas' an' feelin' almighty.

All de sudden, somebody look up on de wall. He stop daid still, an' say, "Jes' looky dere! Dey's a han' writin' up dere on de wall without no awm on hit." An' evuhbody look. Ol' man Bushazzuh look up an' say, "Ah d'clah, iffen dey ain'! Ah'm gittin' out of heah." An' dey all stawted tremblin', but none of 'em knowed whut de writin' say.

Ol' Bushazzuh was wuhrid down in his soul. "Oh, sen' fuh mah lawyuhs. Oh, sen' fuh mah doctuhs, Ah wants to know jes' whut dat writin' about," he say.

An' de lawyuhs come, an' de doctuhs come, an' dey shook dey haids, 'cause dey couldn't read whut hit say. Oh no, Ah say, dey couldn't read whut hit say.

Ol' Bushazzuh say, "Whut do hit mean? Whut do hit mean? Cain't nobody heah tell me whut hit mean?" An' dey tells me dat somebody brung in ol' man Danyul. When ol' man Bushazzuh saw 'im, he say to Danyul, "Danyul, Danyul, kin you read dat dere?"

An' dey tell me ol' Danyul squinted up his eyes. He squinted up his eyes, an' he look real close. Den he stawted in to shake his haid an' say, "Man, you don't want to know whut dat say."

An' dey tell me ol' Bushazzuh look pow'ful wuhrid. "Oh Danyul, Danyul, whut do hit say? Tell me 'cause Ah'm ready to heah anything." Ol' man Bushazzuh knowed he'd been sinnin'.

Ol' Danyul tuhn 'roun' an' shake his haid. "Oh, Bushazzuh, Bushazzuh, has you fuhgot? Has you done fuhgot yo' po' ol' daddy? Don't you 'membuh, man, how de Lawd took away his throne? Don't you 'membuh how dey driv 'im out in de woods? Don't you 'membuh how he growed long haihr all ovuh, an' graze on grass like a mule? Don't you 'membuh dat his tuskies come out like a hawg's? Don't you 'membuh how he growed claws on his han's an' feet? Oh Lawd, oh Lawd. Oh, Bushazzuh, Bushazzuh, you done fuhgot all dat. You done fuhgot dat de Lawd set up kaings an' take away kaings. You fuhgot dat de Lawd change de times an' de seasons. Amen, amen. Oh, Bushazzuh, Bushazzuh, you ain' humblin' yo'se'f befo' yo' Lawd. You is cuttin' hit loose an' lettin' hit swing. You don't evun go to chu'ch on Sunday. You done call yo'se'f so proud an' mighty. You done drunk outten de Lawd's pitchuh an' wuhshipped gol' an silvuh idols 'stead of de Lawd. Ah'd sho hate to be in yo' place, ol' man Bushazzuh, oh, yes Ah would. De Lawd's goin' to cut you off right even with de groun'. Oh, yes, he is. Oh, Bushazzuh, Bushazzuh, de Lawd done writ on de wall 'bout you.

Oh, yes, he has. He done weighed yo' soul an' foun' hit wantin'.
Oh yes, oh yes. Yo' gol' and silvuh might weigh plenty, but yo' soul
done weighed out shawt. Hit don't weigh enough. De Lawd done
took out his scales an' weighed you up. You done shawt weight.
Oh, yes, you is. Amen."

Ol' man Bushazzuh stawted shakin', an' beggin' hawd. He say,
"But, looky heah, Danyul, cain't Ah put on some weight? Whut
mus' Ah do?"

Danyul shook his haid. "Ah'm 'fraid dey ain' nothin' you kin do
now, Bushazzuh. De Lawd done got yo' weight, an' de angels has
put hit down in de book. Hit's too late now. You nevuh weighed
'nough. Dey jes' weighs you once an' don't weigh you no mo'. Oh
no, oh no." Amen.

Hit was a black day fuh ol' man Bushazzuh. Hit was a bad day,
Ah say, when dey weighed him up, an' he nevuh weighed enough.
Amen, amen.

How much does Ah weigh? How much does Ah weigh? Oh chu'ch
oh chu'ch, how much does you weigh? If de Lawd jerks you up
t'night an' puts you on his scales, how much you goin' to weigh?
Is you goin' to bring de awm of de scales down on yo' side, or is
hit goin' to swing you up? How much does you weigh? Has you
suhved yo' Lawd an' he'p put on weight? Or has you set 'roun' jes'
hopin' to weigh enough? Oh Lawd, oh Lawd, how much does Ah
weigh? 'Fo' de meetin's ovuh, an' de ship sail on, let's fin' out how
much do we weigh. Amen. Let's all of us fin' out how much do we
weigh. Let's don't none of us come up too light on dat great day.
Amen.

Ah Is de Way

Chu'ch, de tribe leaduhs has ax me to 'nounce dat dey's goin' to
have dey bahbycue an' chicken dinnuh heah to de chu'ch house,
nex' Friday night. Dey wants to git jes' as many of y'all out fuh de
doin's as dey kin, 'cause dis heah's goin' to be de las' money drive
'fo' de repo't goes in fuh dis yeah. De tribe dat sell de mos' plates
is goin' to git de tribe bannuh fuh dis month.

De vittles ain' goin' to be but two-bits a plate, an' dey tells me
dat dey's goin' to have plenty fuh evuhbody. Let's all git ahr frien's
togethuh an' have a sho 'nough good time nex' Friday night.

Ah'm sho goin' to be dere an' git some of ol' Uncle Luke's bahbycue. You know, Ah been puttin' away Uncle Luke's bahbycue

fuh de las' fifteen yeahs, an' Ah hopes Ah'll be puttin' hit away fifteen yeahs from now. Amen. Ah'll set Uncle Luke up agin 'bout anybody dat evuh come down de pike when hit come to bahbycuin'. Ah sholy will. Ah don' b'lieve de Lawd got any bettuh bahbycuer in Heab'm dan Uncle Luke is. Naw suh. Amen. So let's all tuhn out fuh de bahbycue, an' he'p de tribes raise dey money at de same time. Amen.

Now, iffen dey ain' nothin' else to be tol' 'bout dat bahbycue, Ah think Ah'll git on with mah preachin'.

Ah'm goin' to talk to y'all t'night on "Ah is de Way." De Lawd Jesus done tol' us dat he was de way. De Lawd Jesus tol' de folks dat he is de road to Glory. "Ah is de way." Iffen you is lookin' fuh de highway to salvation, jes' heed whut de Lawd Jesus tell you right dere; 'cause he is sholy de way. An' he is de onlies' way. Amen. De Lawd Jesus done laid out de road. Amen.

You know, iffen a man want to git somewhah, he goin' to ax aroun' an' fin' out whut road will take 'im dere. When he fin' out de right road, he goin' to git on dat road an' go ahaid on it 'til he git dere. If he's smawt an' know he's on de right road, he goin' to stay on dat road, an' not git off. Amen.

Iffen Ah stawts ovuh heah to Sealy, Ah ain' goin' to git on de Catspring road, is Ah? Co'se Ah ain'. 'Cause iffen Ah gits on de Catspring road, Ah ain' goin' to git to Sealy, is Ah? Ah's goin' to git to Catspring instead. Well, amen. Ah ain' goin' to git to Sealy, no mattuh how long Ah stays on de Catspring road, 'cause de Catspring road don' lead to Sealy. Praise de Lawd. Hit lead to Catspring. Praise de Lawd.

"Ah is de way." Yes, Lawd. Now ain't dat fine? De Lawd Jesus done come down heah an' pinted out de road to salvation fuh us. All we got to do is git on dat ol' glory road dat Lawd Jesus pinted out, an' travel right on into Abraham's bosom. Amen. Praise de Lawd.

Ah feels so good 'cause Ah don't have to go 'roun' heah axin' folks de way to glory. De Lawd done had de way all fixed up an' mawked off fuh me. Amen. He done tol' us all what road he want us to take. He done sent down his onlies' begotted son to tell us, "Ah is de way." Well, amen. Chu'ch, he'p me preach.

But hit do beat all how we still gits off de road. We still gits on de wrong road, don't we? Sho we do. Got de road all laid out an' mawked off fuh us, but we still gits off into de by-ways of sin an' devilmint. Amen. Praise de Lawd.

Iffen Ah tol' y'all dat Ah was goin' down to Raccoon Ben' to preach t'night, an' den Ah tuhn 'round an' taken de road to Brenham, folks would say, "Dat man done los' his min'. He call hisse'f goin' to Raccoon Ben', but he done stawted off down de Brenham Road. Dat man's on de wrong road. He got sense 'nough to know de right road, but he done took de wrong road." Yes, dey would. Amen. Folks would sho think dat Ah was plum' crazy. Amen. Shout glory, chu'ch.

Den whut de wul you reckon de Lawd think, when he see us go a-prancin' off down de wrong road to beah pahluhs an' dance halls? 'Specially, since he done taken all de trouble to pint out de right road of Christian livin' to us. Ah 'spect de Lawd gits kin' of put out with us, chu'ch. Amen. Ah 'spect he gits mighty put out with us, sometimes. But praise de Lawd, he always ready to lif' us outten de tanglin' vines of sin, an' set ahr stumblin' feet back on his smooth road to glory. Amen. No mattuh how much we falls off de right road an' go sneakin' off down de wrong road, de Lawd is always dere to he'p us back onto his road agin. Amen. Ain' hit fine, chu'ch? Ain' hit fine, dat Jesus tol' us, "Ah is de way?" Amen, praise de Lawd.

You know, chu'ch, dey ain' nothin' in de wul dat ol' Satan hates like he do de Lawd's road. Satan jes' mighty nigh bile ovuh when he see a Christian chile travelin' de Lawd's road. Yes, he do. He spen' mos' of his time tryin' to figguh out some way to fool us off de Lawd's road. Iffen he kin jes' git a Christian chile off de right road an' onto de wrong road, den he sho 'nough happy. Amen. Praise de Lawd.

Chu'ch, you know, ol' Satan's a rascal. Yes, he is. Ol' Satan'll trick a man iffen he git a half chance, chu'ch. Praise de Lawd. Ol' Satan use evuh sawt of trick in de wul to throw a man off de Lawd's road. He'll set up his signs all along de road, tryin' to fool folks into goin' off down one of his ol' sinful roads. You sho have to watch out fuh ol' Satan's signs, or de fus' thing you knows, you'll be off down one of his by-ways, bogged up past yo' yeahs in some of ol' Satan's sin. Amen. Sho has to watch de road. Yes, we does. Amen.

But we all of us is liable to run off de road, ain' we? Co'se we is. Dere ain' nary one of us dat ain' liable to be fooled offen de road by ol' Satan. He jes' a-strainin' night an' day to lead a Christian chile into de by-ways of sin. Amen. Praise de Lawd.

Well, a-way back yonduh, de Lawd pinted out de road to ol' man Samson. Jesus tol' 'im, "Samson, Ah is de way." An' ol' man Sam-

son went a-travelin' along. He went a-travelin' along de Lawd's own
road. Oh, yes he did, chu'ch. Amen.

Now, dey tells me dat ol' man Samson was a mighty strong man.
When he come to somethin' dat he couldn't go through, he jes' rahr
back and pick hit up an' move hit outten de way. Amen. Yessuh,
he nevuh let nothin' hinduh his trop to glory. He was de Lawd's
own chile, travelin' on down to glory. Amen.

Well, ol' Satan see'd Samson travelin' down de Lawd's road. He
say to hisse'f, "Yonduh's a prayin' chile. Ah got to fool him offen
de Lawd's big road. Ah got to get 'im tuhned off down one of mah
by-ways." Oh, yes, Satan said jes' dat. Amen. Amen.

So ol' Satan set de Philistines' awmy out in Samson's road. Satan tol' 'em, "Boys, stop dat man comin' yonduh. Tuhn 'im off de
road. Oh, tuhn 'im off de road." Dat de way ol' Satan wuck. Git
othuh folks to he'p 'im with 'is devilmint. Amen. Praise de Lawd.

But ol' Samson lit into dem Philistines with a mule's jawbone.
He went right on through dat awmy, like a whirlwin' through a
cawn patch. He kilt so many Philistines, dey had to stawt a new
graveyard to hold 'em all.

Ol' man Samson went travelin' right on down dat road. He say,
"Stan' outten mah way. Stan' outten mah way. Ah's travelin' on
down dis glory road. Ol' Satan bettuh keep hisse'f outten mah road.
Ah'll run right ovuh 'im, as sho as he's bawn. Ah's on de right road,
an' Ah ain' gittin' off. Amen, amen. Oh, Lawd, amen. Stan' outten
mah road, 'cause Ah ain' slowin' up."

Dey tried to stop ol' man Samson by puttin' a house in de road,
but he pick up de house an' kep' a-travelin' right on. Ol' man Samson was a-travelin' de Lawd's road to salvation. Amen, amen.

Ol' Satan nevuh had nobody else to go agin Samson. He tried
to talk de Philistines' awmy into seein' could dey stop Samson onct
mo'. But he wern't talkin' to dem Philistines no mo'. Dey done stood
out in de road an' let Samson hit 'em onct. All dey wanted to do,
was to give 'im all de road dat he wanted. De awmy say, "He done
nigh on kilt us all with a mule's jaw-bone. He liable to have somethin' sho 'nough heavy when he come past us nex' time. We ain'
messin' with dat man no mo'."

Ah say, Samson was a-travelin' long de Lawd's own road. But
he took hit in his haid dat he goin' to have to cote de gals. Ol' Satan was still a-wuckin' at him. Fus' thing you know, Samson done
haulin' a gal along with him. Dat's de quickes' way to git offen de
road. Try to watch de gals, an' try to watch de road. You headin'
fuh trouble sho' nough.

Well, ol' Miss Delilah's sweet talk was what got ol' Samson. Hit tuhn 'im right off de Lawd's own road. He wern't watchin' de road, he was laughin' an' goin' on with Miss Delilah. An' Miss Delilah jes' lead 'im fuhthuh down de wrong road. Po' ol' Samson was on de wrong road. Amen, amen. Oh, praise de Lawd.

Ol' Miss Delilah was a-doin' jes' like Satan tol' huh. He tol' huh to fin' out how come Samson so strong. He knowed he could handle 'im iffen he wern't so strong. He knowed de Philistines could hol' 'im if he wern't so evuhlastin' strong. Amen, amen.

Ol' Miss Delilah stawted beggin' fuh Samson to tell huh. "Man, you de stronges' thing Ah evuh see'd. No wunduh you frailed de daylights outten dem Philistines. How in de wul did you git dat strong? Tell me, Samson, how you got so strong."

But Samson knowed de Lawd nevuh wanted 'im to tell. So he tol' huh dis, den he tol' huh dat. But he sho nevuh tol' huh how he got so strong. Oh no! Oh no! Ol' Miss Delilah wern't studyin' 'bout whut de Lawd wanted. Ol' Miss Delilah was takin' huh awduhs from Satan. Oh, yes, she was. So she kep' on a-beggin' an' a-pickin' at Samson.

'Fo' ol' Samson knowed hit, she done got 'im to tell. He tol' huh dat his haihr was whut made 'im so strong. Den he lay down to take hisse'f a nap. An' Miss Delilah roached his haid plum' bald. She cut evuh haih offen dat man's haid. Oh, yes, she did. Praise de Lawd.

When po' ol' Samson come to, he felt mightly low. He felt too weak to swing a cat. He lay dere an' look aroun' an' say, "Lawd, oh Lawd, what de wul done happened to me? Ah don' b'lieve Ah knows dis road a-tall. Dis ain' de road dat de Lawd pinted out." Po' ol' Samson done on de wrong road.

De Philistines come an' grab 'im an' put out both of his eyes. Den dey hooked him up with a mule, an' dey make 'im wuck. Po' ol' Samson done took de wrong road. Ol' Satan done trick 'im off down a by-way. Amen, amen. Oh, praise de Lawd.

Well, Ah'll tell you, chu'ch, hit looked black fuh ol' Samson. Seem like he'd nevuh see de Lawd's road agin. But de Lawd's always lookin' aftuh his chillun. An' he see'd po' Samson wuckin' like a mule, an' blin' as a bat. An' he see'd po' Samson off down de wrong road. An' he heahed po' Samson a-cryin' to him. He said, "Ah'm goin' to bring dat po' chile back to mah road. Ah'm goin' to let 'im res' in Abraham's bosom." Amen, amen. Oh, chu'ch, de Lawd's de bes' frien' we got.

De Philistines was havin' a celebration one day. All de folks come in from miles a-roun'. Dey was laughin' an' shoutin' an' praisin' ol' Satan. All de bigges' folks in de lan' was dere. An' dey had ol' Samson out, showin' 'im off. "Jes' looky heah what we done got. We done got de stronges' man in de wul. We done chained 'im up with ahr own bahr han's." Oh yes, oh yes.

'Bout dat time de Lawd tetched Samson's haid. De haih growed out like a hoss's mane. Ol' Samson taken de postes dat hel' up de place, unduh each awm. An' den he stawted walkin' back to de Lawd's own road. De whole big meetin' house come fallin' down. Dey wern't nothin' lef' but trash an' cawpsis. Ol' Samson done foun' his way back to de road. Amen, amen. He done on de glory road agin.

Chu'ch, oh, chu'ch, don't lose yo' way. Keep yo' eye on de Lawd's own road. Jesus done tol' you, "Ah is de way." Let's all of us heed whut Jesus say. Amen, amen. Let's all make sho we's on de right road. Oh, praise de Lawd.

IV
Pear Orchard, U.S.A.
A Play in Two Acts
and Nine Characters

IV

When John Henry Faulk took Pear Orchard, U.S.A. on tour in the
early 1970s, the one-man show was inevitably compared to Mark
Twain's stage presentations of an earlier time and to contemporary
actor Hal Holbrook's rendition of Mark Twain Tonight. Like Twain's
characters, the denizens of Faulk's mythical Texas town are verbal
cartoons, drawn larger than life and fleshed out with wit, irony,
and a huge dollop of sentiment. In Faulk's folklorist style, however,
the characters are allowed to speak for themselves. With a change
in voice tone or the way he held his head—and no other props—
Faulk would become a conduit for each of the different personali-
ties and viewpoints. A shift of the spotlight would produce the plum-
my voice of Miss Effie McDoo, complaining how the U.S. Supreme
Court had spoiled her prize sweet peas. A switch of the hand, and
before us is Tom Willis, the Oldest Man in Pear Orchard, refusing
to give in to conformity. Right behind him is Aunt Edith Walters,
measuring her child-raising expertise by her son Toots's success with
the Ku Klux Klan. Each character, including the capacious Fanny
Rollins, who delivers the best gossip in the county, speaks in the
cadence of small-town Middle America with the oral imagery of
tough pioneer ancestors. The rhythm of this speech grows until it
becomes a combination of singing and talking in the blank verse
style of the Reverend Tanner Franklin, a black preacher who delivers
the ending sermon, "David and Goliath," a favorite topic of all country preachers in the South.

Although Pear Orchard, U.S.A. is associated with the Vietnam
and Watergate years, it is actually based on a set of characters developed by Faulk beginning in the 1950s. Early radio and stage ver-
sions were called "Pineville" and "Magnoliaville."

The final stage version presented John Henry Faulk in solo concert, accompanied by a banjo player or guitarist who interspersed
singing and playing folk songs with each of Faulk's characters. All
shared elemental themes of dignity, human rights, race relations,
and simple relations among people who have to struggle to remember who they are and how they got that way. Underlying all of
Pear Orchard, U.S.A. is Faulk's conviction that his small town con-
tains the roots of our complex urban world, that Pear Orchard is
a microcosm of our larger hopes and fears, and that its inhabitants

are pure representations of the national character. In Faulk's America, we will always have a Congressman John Guffaw pressing the flesh and dodging the issues, whether we live in Pear Orchard or Chicago.

Act One

(A medley of rousing patriotic music is playing, climaxing in a verse of "Yankee Doodle" followed by "Dixie." As the music fades, in comes:)

JOHN HENRY FAULK: Hello, I'm John Henry Faulk. Welcome to Pear Orchard. We want you to have a good time tonight. The musician will play you the songs the people in Pear Orchard sing, and I will introduce you to some of the folks and let you hear what they have to say. We figure if you listen to what people talk about and what they sing about, you will get a pretty good impression of them or maybe even understand them.

Actually, there's nothing much to Pear Orchard, it's just an ordinary little town. It's located somewhere between El Paso and Texarkana, the western and eastern extremes of Texas. The Chamber of Commerce down there has a motto: Pear Orchard, U.S.A.—the biggest little town in the country.

Some people might say, "Well, it's a typical town of the Silent Majority." It might be typical of the majority, but there ain't nothing silent about it.

The first time I ever visited the place, I remember it was on Highway 78 where you drive into Pear Orchard, I pulled into a little combination filling station and grocery store that belonged to Ben Rutledge. I wasn't particularly impressed with the place. Ben Rutledge was sitting in a straight-backed chair, leaning against the wall. A little seven- or eight-year-old boy was playing in the driveway with a double-barreled shotgun. That *did* impress me.

I stopped and Ben Rutledge started to get out of his chair and I said, "No, no . . . don't get up. I don't want gasoline, I just want directions. Can you tell me how to get to the County Courthouse?"

BEN RUTLEDGE: Shore can, Mister. I can give you directions a heap cheaper than I can give you gasoline. You couldn't miss it if you wanted to. It's hard to miss the County Courthouse . . . in Pear Orchard.

Albert, honey, Papa's told you not to play with that shotgun like that. It's loaded. I didn't tell you to play with no loaded shotgun.

The County Courthouse is down yonder, like I say. It's been there since 1908, no, no, it was built in 1910, the year my Papa come here . . . it's been settin' there a lot longer than I've been settin' here, I know that.

Albert, now you keep playing with that shotgun and blow your head off, your Mama will wear you out, young man.

A lot of people think that old courthouse oughta be torn down, Mister. Like they say, it has bats in the belfry. I know there was a lawyer here a while back tellin' me that he would defend any man that burned the place down, providing it was a successful job.

Albert, Papa didn't say to point that thing at him. Now quit cocking that thing, honey. Albert, now put down that shotgun and take it back in the house where now you found it—Albert, now put it down!

Uh, like I say, Mister, you can't miss it if you—Albert . . . Mister! Mister! Albert. Don't point loaded shotguns at people, it hurts their feelin's. Well what do you think that man is layin' down on the front seat of that car for?

Mister, don't try to drive off a-layin' down like that, you can't see the road . . . put the gun up, honey . . . Mister, Mister, you go on down to the third red light . . . Yessir, turn right and you'll hit it. Mister, that there light might be green when you get there . . .

(The spotlight switches to the musician, who plays "Bowling Green.")

JOHN HENRY FAULK: The political laurels of Pear Orchard rest on the broad brow of Congressman John Guffaw. Congressman Guffaw is our only claim to fame, and the first citizen of Pear Orchard, at least by his own estimation. He's a proportionate man, with a sense of balance—he's five feet high and almost that wide. Some folks say he's a lot like a baby mockingbird—a whole lot of mouth and very little bird—but those are his detractors.

Congressman Guffaw has been in Congress for the last forty years, so it was quite an event when a barbeque was given in his honor down in Walnut Grove last year, by Congressman Guffaw. Folks gathered under the tall pecan trees, and there was all the barbeque you could hold and all the soda water you could drink.

When the ladies were finished and sitting and fanning themselves with funeral parlor fans, a big truck decorated with red, white, and blue bunting pulled up. The local leader of politics, Mr. Frank Lewis, got up and began to call everyone to order. "Everybody come in close, now. Get in earshot, because our microphone is broke down. We're going to have to do this thing with the nekkid voice. Ladies and Gentlemen, it is my honor to introduce you to that great thinker, that Gibraltar of political integrity, that battler for us all, that Atlas of intellect, our own beloved Congressman John Guffaw!"

CONGRESSMAN JOHN GUFFAW: Fellow Pear Orchardites, I could just reach out and hug and kiss every one of you. It does this old heart of mine so much good to be back down here with the people I love. Oh, I've dined off the golden plates and fine silver of the crowned heads of Europe, and I've et pheasant under glass, but nothing can beat a paper plate full of Texas barbeque down here with the people of Pear Orchard.

You know, my wife often jumps on me and says, "John you love those people in Pear Orchard too much, you sacrifice too much for them. You've got to rest." And I say, "Oh no, honey, you can't love the people of Pear Orchard too much. As long as they deserve me, I aim to serve them."

Before I go any further, though, I want to straighten out a libel that's been issued against me. I want to confess to a charge against me. My opponents have been going around saying John Guffaw loves the Bible too much—he's too religious. John Guffaw loves motherhood too much—he values the American family too much. John Guffaw loves the flag too much—he's too patriotic. I'm back down here today to confess I'm guilty.

But I'm not down here to discuss myself. I'm down here to discuss the burning, vital issues that are before the American people today and particularly the people of Pear Orchard, the people I love. And I'm glad I can discuss these issues honestly. I love the truth, you know. I learned it a long time ago, right here in Pear Orchard, Texas, and I've never been able to shake it since.

I'm glad I can discuss these issues in plain English, the language my mother spoke, the language the Holy Bible was wrote in. I'm glad to be back down here where that old mother of mine once trod. Oh motherhood, motherhood, the sweetest name I know.

Good neighbors, sometimes I think our Maker in His Divine Wisdom, when He saw fit to create His most perfect work, selected this Lone Star State of Texas, this paradise on Earth, came here to the Second Congressional District of this Garden of Eden, and

He caught the gold from the Texas sunrise and He caught the perfume from the Texas bluebonnet, our state flower, then He caught the sweetest notes from the throat of the Texas mockingbird, our state bird, molded it all together, and worked it until He made that most perfect creation of God Almighty: my mother.

Folks, thank you all so much for coming, it's meant a lot to me to discuss these issues with you and I don't want nobody to leave the picnic grounds until I have a chance to shake your hand.

(Music: "This Land is Your Land")

JOHN HENRY FAULK: One of the oldest men living in Pear Orchard is Mr. Tom Willis. Tom Willis looks exactly like what he is—an old Texas cattleman. His father went up the trail with the herds in the days when they had to drive the cattle up to Kansas to get them to the railroad.

Mr. Tom Willis lives alone. His wife has been dead about twenty years. He's over eighty and still active. He does all his own cooking, keeps his own house, and drives his own car. But most important of all, Mr. Tom Willis does his own thinking. When I need my mental batteries charged up, I always go sit down with Mr. Tom on his front porch and talk.

I was sitting over there the other day talking about the fact that the Fourth of July was coming up soon, while he crumbled up corn bread and tossed it to some Dominecker chickens out in the yard. I said, "You know, I was just reading that when the Continental Congress approved the Declaration of Independence on July 4, 1776, the people of Philadelphia poured into the streets with singing and dancing. Bells rang for twenty-four hours. I would like to believe, Mr. Tom, that we Americans today could recapture that same excitement over the idea that free men can govern themselves."

TOM WILLIS: Johnny, you know, that there worries me a heap. By God, it seems that people don't quite know what it's all about no more. Them that talks loudest is the ones that seem to know the least.

Now you take that nephew of mine, Buck. He come over here the other day in that new Chevrolet pickup truck of his. That truck had six bumper stickers—three on the front and three on the back—and all said the same thing: "America—Love It or Leave It." He brung along an extra one and wanted to put it on my car.

I said, "Buck, I don't want that fool motto on my car."

He swole up and said, "What's the matter? Don't you believe in patriotism?"

I said, "Buck, I don't know everything about patriotism, but I know what it ain't. It ain't goin' around intimidatin' your neighbors. That thing don't even mean what it says. It says, 'America— Love It or Leave It' but what it really means is 'Agree with me or I'll knock your teeth down your throat.' "

Well! Buck started swelling some more. He said, "Uncle Tom, you better be careful, or people going to take you for one of them old effete snobs. Our leaders up in Washington got their eyes on such as you, and they don't appreciate that kind of fancy talk."

I said, "Buck, let me tell you about those boys up in Washington. By God, they work for me. I don't work for them. They come to me and my neighbors three years ago and said, 'Give us a job a-driving this old American bus.' They said they had the blueprint and the road map and promised they could drive us to peace and prosperity. They said they knowed every crook and turn, and would drive us along a smooth highway.

"Well, we give them the job. Then they started to driving. Now when they keep a-driving off the road and a-getting off down in the bushes and a-throwing her in reverse and a-stalling the engine and the womenfolk are nervous and the children all a-crying, I just retch up and tap the boys on the shoulder and say, 'Boys, get back up there on the highway where you promised us you was going to drive at.'

"Buck, I don't want the Washington boys a-turning around and saying, 'Get off the bus if you don't like our driving.' By God, it's *my* bus. They're just the temporary drivers."

Well, that made old Buck mad. He jumped up and said, "You better put one of these here bumper stickers on your car so people won't know how ignorant you are."

I said, "Buck, I might be ignorant but I shore ain't going to drive around town with a sign on my car advertising the fact."

Well, he got in his pickup, started the motor, revved it up, shook his fist out the window at me, and said, "Me and the Silent Majority will take care of you."

I said, "Buck, when you and the boys up in Washington run your next poll on the Silent Majority, if you come up minus one—it's me."

(*Music: "Reuben James"*)

JOHN HENRY FAULK: The nearest thing we have to a social register in Pear Orchard is the Pear Orchard Garden Club. It meets the third Thursday of each month. Every lady who is anybody in Pear Orchard belongs. They gather to talk about who's getting married, who's likely to get married, who ought to get married, and sometimes flowers.

I went because I was interested in hearing the guest speaker from over in Pinedale, Miss Effie McDoo. Miss Effie is known as Miss Sweet Pea of Texas.

Before her talk on "The Care and Culture of Sweet Peas," Miss Effie was introduced by Linda Swenson, president of the garden club, who called her the very essence of knowledge on sweet peas. Miss Effie McDoo stood there at first, properly modest, and then her face creased into a magnificent smile that warmed the entire room, every nook and cranny of it.

MISS EFFIE: Girls of the Pear Orchard Garden Club, it's just a glorious adventure to be with you here today. I don't think braver and newer things are being done anywhere in the garden club world than are being done right here.

You asked me to come here to speak on the care and culture of the sweet pea, but I'm afraid I'm not going to speak on that today. Instead, my talk is on civil rights—the civil rights of sweet peas. And two words will explain the whole challenge: Supreme Court.

You may say, "Well, the Supreme Court hasn't been stomping around your sweet pea beds!" No, girls, I have to tell you a story:

I don't have sweet peas, not even one this year. I know that comes as a shock to so many of you. All of you who know me very well, know that I have this wonderful old darkie, a yardman, Uncle Cy, who has been with us now for thirty-seven years. Why, my husband, Lee, often teases me and says, "Uncle Cy ought to get part of the first prizes you win for your sweet peas 'cause he does all the work!"

I also have what you might call a "sweet pea neurosis." I have to have my sweet peas in the ground the week before Christmas, or I won't put them in the ground at all. I know a lot of you-all like to put them in the ground in the fall, and some of you put them in the ground in late February. I just have to have mine in by Christmas—I want them to be asleep when Santa Claus comes.

Yes, girls, the week before Christmas finally arrived, the time that Uncle Cy had come to work for the past thirty-seven years.

But no Uncle Cy came. I asked my maid, Maple, "Where in the world is Uncle Cy? This is the week, this is the day, to put the sweet peas in the ground." She said, "Didn't you hear, Miss Effie? Uncle Cy passed away in late October." Well, girls, I was shocked.

I said, "I certainly didn't hear about it. He didn't send word to me to that effect." You know as good as you are to them, they will treat you this way. You can't depend on them. They're children at heart. I don't think Lee has thrown away an old pair of shoes in the past thirty-seven years that Uncle Cy didn't get first bid on them. That old man just adored Lee's shoes.

Well, I decided I didn't come from old Texas pioneer stock for nothing. I was going to get those sweet peas in the ground in spite of Uncle Cy. So I got hold of the county agent. He told me where I could find a young man who had taken an agriculture course and I went out there to get him. He was a darkie, too, you know. He had eight or nine pickaninnies around the yard. He didn't want to come until the next day, but I said "No, we're going to get those peas in the ground today," and I brought him in.

Girls, he got out there in my garden and started working. I don't know if you have ever had the exhilarating experience of having someone in your beds who knows exactly what he is doing. It's just glorious. I went around the house all day, just so excited. I'd look out the window and see him working and I neglected my own Christmas wrapping and everything else.

And you know, when I was in college at Ward Belmont, I was going to be a concert pianist. Beethoven and Wagner and all those big musicians came through there and urged me to continue with my music. But I got married and gave it up. But that day I was inspired. I just went to the piano and played several pieces I hadn't played in the longest time—Wagner's "To an Evening Star" and others. My maid thought I had gone crazy, but I was just exhilarated and happy.

Then the young man came to the door that afternoon and wanted his money. I said, "But you haven't got the sweet pea frames up yet!" And he said, "I'd like to get today's pay 'cause one of the children is sick." You know, they always have some excuse like that.

So, against my better judgment, I said, "Will you be here first thing in the morning?" He said, "Yes, I'll be here at daylight and finish the job. I need some money for Christmas, and I need some medicine for the children."

I paid him. I opened my purse and paid him the money.

He stood there in the kitchen and—I never will forget—he looked at that fifty-cent piece and that quarter and said, "Madam, is this my day's pay?" I said, "Yes," in all innocence, you know. His eyes narrowed, his nostrils flared, and he flung the coins on the floor.

He said, "Madam, I do believe you need the money worse than I do." And he turned around and hurtled out the door, slamming it in my face.

Girls, I had heard of black power, but I never thought I'd see it in my kitchen. It just shocked me. I had never seen violence before that. Oh, my grandfather down there on his place used to have lynchings. But I had never seen black power violence. I was so shocked I sat down at the table.

I was still shaking when Lee came home. I told him the whole story. Lee just sat there and drummed his fingers on the table and said, "Honey, I could have told you that was going to happen."

I said, "Lee, what do you mean, you could have told me something like that was going to happen in my home?"

He said, "Don't you know there are no more Uncle Cy's? That Supreme Court has gone and passed laws about people voting and having to go to school together and drinking from the same water fountain. But we know it ain't got nothing to do with people going to school together. It's got to do with not being able to get darkies to work for seventy-five cents a day no more."

I looked at him, girls, and I said, "Lee, where in the world is red-blooded American manhood today that just sits back and allows the Supreme Court to run loose in this country?"

He looked at me and he said, "Woman, what in the world do you think we have been doing? We did our best to get that old Earl Warren impeached. We liked to have got that done, but he quit on us, and every bunch since then has been the same. What do you want us to do about it?"

I said, "The least thing you could do is get together and deport them."

"Honey," Lee told me, "I'd just forget them. The Supreme Court of the United States has pulled the same stunt all these radicals pull these days: they come here and get themselves born and you can't deport them."

So, girls, I don't have any sweet peas this year. I'm not sure I'm planting any again, until I know that America will be safe for the sweet pea.

(Music: "Royal Baking Powder")

JOHN HENRY FAULK: It doesn't get cold very often down in Pear Orchard. But when it does, a blue norther usually sweeps in and turns everything icy. One bitter, freezing morning I was driving along the county road when I saw a boy walking ahead of me. He was about ten or twelve years old, wore ragged overalls, and the sleeve of an old coat was tied around his ears. I stopped to pick him up and when he got in the car, I noticed he was barefoot. His feet were blue with cold. I said, "Son, you ought to have on shoes in weather like this."

BOY: Ain't got no shoes, Mister. Heat sure feels good, though, I'll tell you that. None of us young 'uns got shoes out to our place. Papa always says he feels like he's lucky to keep clothes on our backs without worrying about shoes for our feet. There's eight of us children, you know. We never do think about shoes much, except my sister Lois Irene.

She's been thinking about them a heap, lately. She's seventeen, and she got a job working for a lady. She told Mama she's going to save up her money for a pair of shoes. Lois Irene said she'd give a purty if she had a pair of shoes to wear down to church.

Every afternoon she'd come home from that lady's house and tell us something wonderful about that lady and her two children that Lois Irene took care of.

She said there was two sheets on every bed in that house. She said that lady would have her set up at the table and they had this bread that's done sliced like you see at a Sunday school picnic. She said that lady told her to help herself, to put all the butter on it she wanted.

One Saturday afternoon she come home and said that there lady had give her something she had wrapped in a newspaper. She wouldn't tell us what it was till we done ate supper. When we had all ate, Mama she turned the lamp up and Lois Irene she unwrapped it. It was the purtiest pair of ladies' shoes you ever seen. Mama said, "Honey, where did you ever git all the money?" Lois Irene said that lady just give them to her for nothing 'cause she was tired of wearing them herself.

She took them over to Papa where he was sitting on the bed. Papa, he's blind, but he said he didn't believe he never felt no shoes nicer than that. Then Lois Irene put them on and showed just how ladies walk in them. She walked back and forth.

She told me and my brother Ernie that we could go to Sunday school with her the next day, that she was going to wear the shoes down to church. And, boy, that night we couldn't hardly sleep. We just lay there giggling about Lois Irene wearing the shoes.

We got up the next morning and me and Ernie put on our clean overalls. Mama, she combed out Lois Irene's hair real purty and got out that purty dress she has for Lois Irene.

And Lois Irene went to get her shoes to put on, but they wasn't there.

My little brother Leroy was playing with them down close to the wash place. He didn't know what they was, he hadn't never seen ladies' shoes before. He was playing choo-choo with them.

When we found them, the left shoe's heel had done been broke off. Papa said if we could find that heel, he could get it back on there 'cause the nails were still in the shoe. So we started hunting up under the house and everywhere we figured Leroy likely played at. But we couldn't find it. Pretty soon Lois Irene just sat down on the back porch next to Papa and she couldn't hardly keep from crying.

We give up on it. Mama was standing there with the baby in her arms, and me and old Ernie sat down on the porch, too.

Papa, he was holding on to them shoes, and all of a sudden we seen a smile come on his face. He said, "Bring me that old spool that the coarse thread come on. I've got a notion."

Mama brung him that spool. Papa, he felt that heel that's still on one shoe and he started whittling on that spool. The next thing you know, he whittled it out just as smooth. He held that shoe between his knees and tapped that spool on there. And Mama, she put stove blacking on it and you couldn't tell one shoe from the other.

Well sir, Lois Irene was a-hugging Papa and me and Ernie at the same time. So Papa told her, "Now, I wouldn't try to wear them shoes all the way down to church. That heel might work off. If I was you, I'd pack them in my hands till I got purty near down there."

So we struck out on the road, me and Ernie alongside Lois Irene. She was packing them shoes and walking barefoot like us. And when we got near to church, Lois Irene she went behind a clump of cedar bushes and she slipped them shoes on, just as the last folks was going in to sit down.

And the choir commenced to singing and me and Ernie and Lois Irene walked up there and Lois Irene pushed open the door and she went a-walking through. Her hair was just shiny and brown down her back. The folks was all standing up singing, and the preacher was leading them.

Lois Irene started walking right up the aisle. Me and Ernie was right behind her. She was walking in them there shoes, all the way up to the front pew. She sat down and me and Ernie slipped in there beside her. We couldn't hardly get our breath.

Like I say, shoes ain't important, I guess. Unless you ain't got none.

(Music: "God Bless the Child")

INTERMISSION

Act Two

JOHN HENRY FAULK: When I want an authoritative report on most any subject, I always stop by and see Mrs. Edith Walters. The other day I went out to visit her, and she declared that nobody cared how children were raised anymore. That was what was wrong with the country today, she said.

I said, "Miss Edith, I think you're rather incorrect about that. As a matter of fact, I don't remember a time when so much attention was given to child-raising, when more books were written, more lectures delivered. It seems to me we live in a period when more is known about child-raising than ever before.

MRS. EDITH WALTERS: Honey, that there is where you just opened your mouth and stuck both feet in it, as far as I'm concerned. Child-raising! People don't raise children no more!

Look at them old long-haired hippies, wearing them tacky old clothes and a-beating on them guitars. Look at what's going on at the University of Texas. Just a cesspool of nastiness and atheism, is all. If a child goes up there with a little raising, they'll take it right out of him. Those old atheistic professors will make him march in protests and get violent, or they won't give him a passing mark. Thank God, I raised my two boys and never had to put up with such ugliness.

My first baby was little old Toots. Me and Rip thought so much of Toots, bless his heart. When he was three and a half years old, Willy was born. Rip used to have so much fun with little old Toots, he'd say, "Now, you'd better behave yourself, young man, we don't need you no more. We got another baby now. We'll throw you to the hogs."

Lordy! It would make little old Toots so mad. He'd hold his breath and beat his little old head on the floor. Of course, I'd whip him as soon as he did that.

Toots always had it in for Willy. When the baby was eight months old, Toots got at him with a pine knot and hit him in the mouth. Thank goodness, Willy didn't have no teeth or Toots would have knocked them out.

Rip come home that night and said, "Well, sir, you just carried it a bit too far. I'm going to lock you in the corncrib and let them old gray rats eat you." He did, and little Toots just ripped and snorted and hollered. I told Rip, "We ain't going to get no sleep the way he's a-carrying on."

So Rip went out there and gave him a good whipping and brought him in and for a long time after that, Toots had a real flair for showing off. He'd just kind of jerk all over.

That Toots was smart as a briar. By the time he was six years old, he could say his alphabet right down to M and N. He'd ride over to the Magnolia schoolhouse on that notch-eared mule, and come home every afternoon, squalling. Them big old boys at the schoolhouse boxed his jaws till his ears rung.

One night Rip got tired of it and took out that old skinning knife he had, that old Dallas special of his. It had a button on it, and it would throw out a blade that long. He always kept it razor sharp. He showed little Toots how to hold it and how to throw that blade.

Next day, little old Toots went off to school, proud of that knife in his overalls pocket. At recess, he started out to the bushes to relieve himself—Toots always had a weak bladder, and wet the bed until he was twenty-two years old—and the two oldest Grogan boys and that hateful Simpson kid jumped on him. They backed him up against the wall of the schoolhouse and started slapping his little old jaws.

Well, Toots put his hand in his pocket and he throwed that blade and started slicing. He cut that oldest Grogan boy plumb to the heart, his entrails dropped out like a shoat at hog-killing time. And what tickled me most, he hit that old Simpson boy. Cut loose all the ligaments in his hand. That was thirty years ago, but you go down to the Sinclair station in Pear Orchard, and you can see his fingers is still standing out.

When little old Toots come home, he was the proudest thing. He was covered in blood, but he didn't want me to wash his overalls or anything.

Of course, everybody said he was going to turn out bad. But Toots ain't. Toots has gone up in the world. He worked for the Southern Pacific Railroad for a while, but he don't do that no more. He's retired now, honey. He lives over in Arkansas where he's head of the whole Ku Klux Klan there. But he set up a separate organization, now. It's called the HHA—the Hippie Hunters of America. Oh, if you let one of those hippies come near Toots, he's after him. Yessiree, Toots don't allow nobody to be violent around him.

(Music: "There Was an Old Man")

JOHN HENRY FAULK: I found a new friend down in Pear Orchard while looking for a rocking chair. The local furniture store clerk told me they didn't stock rockers anymore, but said if I would drive out to see Miss Fanny Rollins, she might have one that she had no more use for.

When I arrived at her mailbox, I could see a long, oleander-bordered walkway leading up to the front porch of a country farm home. A woman was sitting in a porch swing taking up room for four people. That capacious soul was spread all over the swing, her arms resting on her ample bosom, which went all the way around to her backbone, just like a hen fixing to fly off a low roof. I said, "How do you do, ma'am. I'm looking for Miss Fanny Rollins."

MISS FANNY: Heh, heh. Well, honey, you'd better get an eye doctor if you can't see her. I've been accused of a heap of things, but being invisible ain't one of them. Have a chair, sit down. That little rocker? Yes, it is a nice one. No, I wouldn't be interested in selling it. Oh, no. It's funny you mention it, because my daughter-in-law Bertha Mae, Gervis's wife, was over here the other day asking for it. Of course, I can't set in it at all, now. It would take three of them to hold me.

Bertha Mae's a sweet girl. And talented! Folks don't know it, but—bless her heart—she can rub her stomach and pat her head and recite all the books of the Bible backwards. And stop right in the middle to whistle a spiritual. Even preachers can't do that. All her family was talented that way.

Her oldest brother, Fred, he's one-armed. I don't know how he lost his arm, it was either in a hay-baler or a car accident, but I know it was an accident. He didn't do it on purpose. He had a 1952 pickup truck and a double hernia and he could train dogs like nobody I seen. Had that old blue-tick hound named Scooter. He was three-legged, and ever so often people would say, "I wonder why God left that dog's hind leg off him?"

God has a purpose. Most dogs, you know, have to slow down to smell around a bush. Well, Scooter scarcely had to pause. He'd do his business and be gone. Fred had him trained to carry a milk bucket. Fred, being one-armed, couldn't pack two buckets of milk at the same time, so Scooter carried the other. Wouldn't spill a drop. Fred had him trained to where he would say, "Scooter! The wood box is empty," and Scooter would get up, go trotting out to that woodpile on three legs, pick up a mouthful of kindling, and come drop it in the wood box.

You know, it's a funny thing, I give Scooter a heap of credit, but not for good judgment when it comes to dynamite and wood. There was a road construction crew working out there one day and Scooter came trotting in with a stick of dynamite. Dropped it in the wood box. And Fred, absent-minded-like, stuck it in the stove.

I'll say this, it was as interesting a funeral as we ever had here. Never found nothing but Fred's left shoe, and his foot was still in it. The family went down to Cartwright's Funeral Parlor and asked for a left-foot coffin. Cartwright said they didn't stock them. Well, they argued back and forth for the longest time and the family finally settled for buying the whole coffin. I thought it was amusing to see—a coffin big enough for a whole corpse, with just a left foot in it.

All of that family was talented like that. Take that little old Annie Lee. Oh, that was a sweet little thing. But she had a lot of tragedy. When she was about thirteen years old, she went out to the barn to milk the cows and there come up a thunderstorm. Lightning struck her right between the eyes. It soured both buckets of milk. Electricity is strange. It give that child a terrible headache. They thought at first that's all it did, but it turned out to have straightened her hair.

Oh, bless her little old heart, she tried to get it curly again. She put it up in paper curlers and left it up for thirty-six days in a row as a trial run. She took the curlers out, run her comb through it, and it was straight as a horse's tail. 'Course that ain't all lightning will do to you—it flattened that child's chest. Well, honey, I ain't talking about being just flat-chested, she was ironing-board flat-chested.

But she went to town and got her a job working at the state highway department. Saved her money and bought her a pair of foam-rubber bosoms. Oh, it changed her whole outlook on life. Annie Lee got to where she'd come to church twice on Sunday. Even started singing in the Methodist choir, and she had no more voice than a white leghorn pullet.

It was all because of the bosoms. And she started coming to our quilting parties every Friday. We had a little old Methodist preacher named Brother Walker, he'd stand there while we quilted, hoorah-ing with us ladies. Annie Lee was setting at the frame behind me. Brother Walker, he was laughing and chatting, and all of a sudden his jaw went slack, sweat popped out on his brow, and his eyes rolled back in his head. I thought he was having a fainting spell. I said, "Brother Walker, are you well?" He didn't answer me at all, he just grabbed the doorknob and went through the door mumbling, "Oh Lord, oh Lord." I turned my eyes and understood the whole thing. Annie Lee was using that left bosom as a pincushion. She'd run that big old Number 9 needle clear through from one side to the other.

Annie Lee kept on using those bosoms until she found Totsie Taylor and married him. But she still had a lot of tragedy, honey. Totsie was a-setting on the railroad tracks one day, just a-thinking of something, when the Katy Flyer came by at 700 miles an hour and hit him. Well, I say hit him. It exploded him. He was setting there one minute and the next he was a puff of mist floating across the field. They estimated his remainders floated over two and a half acres. The family leased about four acres for the funeral, just to be safe. The pallbearers all had a turn at the plow. Brother Culpepper came from Liberty Hill and said it was the biggest funeral he ever preached. Acreage-wise.

Brother Culpepper always knowed the right thing to say. You know, he preached Papa's funeral. Papa passed away sitting in that little rocker that you're in right now. He had such a quiet passing, I didn't know he was gone, to tell the truth. One afternoon, I was shelling black-eyed peas in my lap. Just a-chatting and a-talking to him and he'd grunt every once in a while. After a while, I didn't notice him a-grunting. I looked up and he was gone. No death rattle, no struggle. His head just dropped forward. Drop your head forward, honey. Now let it hang down. There, just like that. I've always said I ain't no scientist, but if that had been a straight chair, Papa would have come out of it and I would have knowed he was dead. Straight chair won't hold a corpse. But Papa's body just rocked back in that little rocker. That's the reason, honey, I wouldn't sell it for anything in the world. It's got sentimental value to it.

(Music: "Careless Love")

JOHN HENRY FAULK: There is one more citizen down in Pear Orchard of whom I am very fond. The Reverend Tanner Franklin lives out on a farm, not far from the area where his folks were freed from bondage. Reverend Tanner Franklin is six and a half feet tall, farms all week, and preaches on Sunday in the old Shiloh Baptist Church, a tiny little church down under the cypress trees in the bottomlands along the river.

Reverend Tanner Franklin can't read or write. But he has leaned his ear over close to the earth and has caught the rhythms and the sounds of the earth. There's not a wild bird that nests in all that area that he can't identify by its song. There's not a wildflower that blossoms in his fields that Reverend Tanner Franklin can't hold up to his nose and give its folk name.

Reverend Tanner Franklin is all the more remarkable because he is one of the few men I've ever encountered who is completely free from those limitations that most of mankind has, namely bigotry and prejudice. He is too big for that, has too spacious a soul.

And on the Sunday night I'd like for you to meet him, the congregation of some eighteen or twenty people were gathered by the light of a single lantern hanging from the cross beam over the pulpit, singing an old song. And this old song went:

> You've got to stand up, you've got to stand up,
> You've got to stand up to get the job did.
> You've got to stand up, you've got to stand up,
> You've got to stand up, you gonna move ahead.

As that old song ebbed and flowed and ebbed and flowed and died away in a long hum, Reverend Tanner Franklin stood up there in the lantern light and said:

REVEREND FRANKLIN: Well, glory, church, that's the song I love. It

tells just what we got to do in this old world if we're going to make
it on through. We got to stand up and move on ahead. We can't
just sit here and study about it all the time. Amen.

Well, now church, in the imagination of my mind I want to take
you all way back yonder to Bible times.

I see over one slope of the hill the Philistine army all gathered
up in battle raiment.

Down across a little creek and over yonder slope of the hill was
the Israelite army.

They were having a battle, and neither side winning and neither
side losing.

You going to say to me, well, why wasn't the Israelite chillun,
God's chosen people, prevailing in the battle?

Church, I have to report to you tonight that the Israelite army
was led by an old sit-down-and-do-nothin' by the name of King Saul.

He didn't get up to fight God's battle.

He sat there and studied about it all the time.

Well, now, church, in the imagination of my mind, I want to
carry you all to a meadowland.

I see the sheeps grazing 'round on the green grass, butterflies and
bees visiting with the flowers, mockingbirds singing in the treetops.

And sitting in the shade of a tree was a sweet little shepherd boy
named David, playing on his harp, singing psalms to the Lord and
minding his daddy's sheep.

Church, I see old man Jesse, little David's daddy, when he come
hobbling out that morning, callin':

"My son David, your mama's fixed up some clean clothes and
vittles for your brothers that's fighting down agin those old mean
Philistines.

"Chile, would you take them down to 'em?"

Church, I see that obedient shepherd boy David when he got in
the buggy,

Slap the mule across the back and strike out for the battlefield,

Get off down there at the battlefield and say "Whoa, mule,"

Hitch the reins around one wheel of the buggy and come crawl-
ing out,

Look over the battlefield, walk up to a big Israelite soldier and say:

"Cousin So-and-So, I thought you all had a battle going on here,
This here don't look like a battleground to me, look more like a

Sunday school picnic ground to me. I don't see nary a lick being struck."

Israelite soldier run his arm around little David, he say, "Baby, look across that creek over there, there among the Philistines.

"See that big tall thing stickin' up like a mountaintop?

"Chile, that ain't no mountaintop, that's that old Philistine giant man Goliath.

"He wants to fight the biggest warrior we got, and we ain't got nary a biggest one this morning."

Church, they tell me that morning something started moving in little David's heart.

He stole down there to the tent where old King Saul was sitting there, holding his head in his hands.

He wasn't up fighting God's battle, he was sitting there studying about it.

Hummmmmm.

Little David stole in there:

"King Saul!

"Well, King Saul, if don't nobody else want to fight that giant man Goliath, let me have a go at it.

"He might look like tall timber to you boys,

"But he look like brush to me,

"And I'll chop him off even with the ground this morning."

Church, old King Saul said, "Go ahead on, fight him, honey, we're going to lose the war anyhow."

But little David wasn't thinking that way.

He walked down to the creek and selected himself five smooth stones, and all alone and by himself, church—now, mind you—all alone and by himself that chile David started stealing up the slope yonder toward the Philistine army.

Now, hear me, church.

The mightiest force the world had ever seen at that time was all arrayed up yonder amongst the Philistines.

And little David marched on up there,

All alone and by himself,

With just a purpose in his mind.

Old man Goliath was a-marching around there, a-talking big.

Oh, he was a giant man, so many cubits high I can't number them all.

He was carrying a sword in his hand longer than a wagon tongue,
And a shield on his arm bigger than a housetop.
He raised his big old ugly foot up,
And stomped the ground real hard, it shook acorns off the trees
'way over in the next county.
Oh, that giant man spied little David coming up the slope,
And said, "Now who sent a shirttail young 'un to do battle with
me?
"Chile, you better turn around and get home to your mama.
"I'll step on you and not leave enough for the buzzards to pick."
Up in Zion that morning, church, God got word that His chile
David was fighting His battle for Him.
Called the angels together and said:
"Move around heaven and find me a bright rainbow to wear
around my neck for a scarf this morning.
"Hush the winds down in the four corners of the Earth.
"Stand the Sun still in the heavens where it's at,
"And some of you angels bend low with your wing tips and sweep
the skies clear.
"I want a clear view, a clear view of my chile David,
"Fighting my battle for me down there this morning."

Church, as the Lord and His angels peeked down over the bat-
tlements of glory, little David slipped a smooth stone in his sling-
shot and he started winding up.
Old man Goliath says, "Boy, I told you not to wind that thing
up at me that way."
About that time little David caught him right between the eyes
with a rock.
Whop!
And that giant man measured his length out on the ground.
The Philistines, seeing it, fled over the hilltops and in fear and
trembling disbursed and have not returned since,
Nor been heard of to this day.
Little David walked up there and took that big sword off of that
giant man,
And sawed his ugly head off with it.
The Israelite army all came a-running and a-shouting glory,
And said, "Little David's a hero!"
But little David said, "No such a thing. All I did is get up and
move on ahead.

"God wants them in this world to get up and get the job did,
"Not just sit there and study about it."

Amen.

V
The Great American Opinion Poll

V

The opinion poll is the constant companion of American humor, offering endless possibilities for spoofing interviewee and subject at the same time, with the pollster as the innocent straight man. John Henry Faulk polished his polls on radio, on both CBS and National Public Radio, on television, in newspaper columns, and over decades of speaking engagements. His specialty is the interview that seems to begin with a simple question and ends up galloping away with poll, pollster, and pollee. These selections from Faulk's polls include the famed monologue by Cousin Ed Snodgrass, "Leave Lyndon Alone and Let Him Fight His War in Peace."

The Great American Opinion Poll

Hello, I'm John Henry Faulk. I've been taking a public opinion poll. You know, that's the style these days: if the polls show you percentages that are on this side or that side of an issue, why, you're home safe. Now, my poll is not like Harris or Gallup. I'm not scientific like they are. But my poll is in depth. I take it one person at a time.

With everybody in Washington these days talking about whether or not Nixon should be impeached, I thought you all might be interested in a little poll I took down home in Texas. I took it among the silent majority, whom I've discovered are no longer very silent.

My first pollee was Mr. Hudson, a sweet old man. I said, "Mr. Hudson, what do you think about this subject of impeachment?"

He said, "Johnny, I ain't got much opinion on impeachment. I don't understand the process. It's beyond me. But I will say this: if it's got anything to do with getting rid of Dick Nixon, I'm for it."

My second pollee was Mrs. Berty Cully. She was ninety years old, and I knew that she disliked Nixon intensely. I was astonished at her response when I asked, "Miss Cully, how do you feel about impeaching Dick Nixon?"

"I'm dead set agin it," she snapped.

"You're against it? Why, I thought you would approve. Why are you against impeachment?"

"Because I had experience with people like Nixon. It's the same trouble we had with my brother Frank's old hunting dog, Lefty.

Lefty was a good hunter and a good hound. But he had a character defect. Lefty was a chicken-killer. Frank threatened him, whupped him, reasoned with him—tried everything, but he couldn't break Lefty from chicken-killin'. Oh, Lefty would swear off and go on the wagon for a couple of weeks. Then a crisis would come along and next thing you knew Lefty had kilt another chicken. He would feel terrible about it and go on the wagon again for a spell. But it wouldn't last.

"About a year ago, Frank come over to have breakfast with me and brought Lefty. Lefty was laying out there on the back porch, resting. Frank says to me, 'You know, ol' Lefty has took the cure. He ain't touched a feather on a chicken for nearly six months.'

"At that very minute, one of my Dominecker hens started across the backyard to the water trough. Lefty spied her, started trembling all over, and you could see him fightin' back temptation. His willpower wasn't up to the test. In a flash he was onto that hen. Minute later there was feathers flyin' around the yard and the hen layin' there with a broke neck.

"Lefty dropped his ears, shame wrote in his face. He laid down, lolled out his tongue, and started beating his tail in the dust, waiting for his whupping. Frank went out an' says, 'Lefty, I ain't going to whup you this time. This time I'm going to cure you.' Then Frank got a piece of wire and he wired that dead hen to Lefty's neck.

" 'Now sir,' Frank tells him, 'You're going to wear that hen till you wear her out.' "

"Well sir, I've knowed a lot of dogs in my life. Heaps of them. But I never knowed a dog that lost friends as fast as Lefty did with that chicken around his neck. His popularity got plumb down to zero. Wasn't a dog in this county that would let Lefty git in barking distance of him.

"Two weeks later, after that hen got good and ripe and dropped off Lefty's neck, he was a cured dog. He had took the cure and took it for good. You can just bring up the subject of chicken around Lefty now, and he'll crawl so far back under the house that you can't coax him out for a week.

"That's why I don't want to see Dick Nixon impeached. I think we ought to wire him around the Republikins' necks and make them wear him till it breaks them of nominating such people."

While I was out taking my poll, a society lady came over to see me. She was a terribly sweet soul, but she was all upset. She had just had a shocking experience, she said.

"Johnny, you know I was visiting with my nephew, the sweetest little boy, oh, he's a darling. His daddy is a colonel in the air force and just the grandest man in the world. I used to take his daddy to Sunday school with me. I called him Tootsie Man and he called me Aunt Boo. Isn't that sweet? But he grew up and learned to fly airplanes and he went off and became a pilot over there in Vietnam. And he'd fly those big old B52 bombers, 'way up in the air. He said you could hardly breathe up there, it was so high. You know, it was just so dramatic and romantic and everything being a pilot.

"He said when he was carrying those bombs over the country down below, he would remember our Sunday school and he would say, 'Aunt Boo would be proud of me.' And when he pressed the button, he would always say a little prayer, hoping that those bombs fell where they were supposed to fall and did what they were supposed to do. Tootsie Man always believed in prayer.

"Well, bless goodness, his little son, Emmet Lee Junior, was over at the house the other day. He's just twelve years old, and he said, 'Aunt Boo, do you think I could be president of the United States?' Johnny, do you know what I told him? It just burst out of me. I said, 'Honey, I hope not. I'd rather see you pick cotton. I'd rather have you take up bank robbing. I'd rather see almost anything happen to you than have you go try to be a good president of the United States. I know we used to tell our little boys to try to become president when they grew up, but today the world is such that every time we get a fine and noble president in the White House, the first thing old mean people do is try to impeach him. And I wouldn't want that to happen to you, little Emmet.' Bless his heart. He looked up at me and said, 'You're thinking about Mr. Nixon, aren't you, Aunt Boo?' And I said, 'Yes, honey, the presidency's not safe for good people any more.' "

Leave Lyndon Alone
and Let Him Fight His War in Peace

I went out to see Cousin Ed Snodgrass the other day. He's an old, dyed-in-the-wool southerner. Cousin Ed has a motto: "Yankee beware. Robert E. Lee might have give up, but I ain't."

He's just as bad about Texas, thinks the sun rises and sets in Texas. He goes around running his mouth all the time about Texas being the biggest state in the Union, and says he'll fistfight the man who says it's not.

I told him he would have to quit talking like that. People will just laugh in his face because everyone knows Alaska is bigger than Texas.

"I don't recognize Alaska," he said.

I said, "Well, that just makes you look even more idiotic because it's there and it's almost twice the size of Texas and that just shows you how absurd you are."

Cousin Ed replied, "If Dean Rusk and Lyndon Johnson and the boys up in Washington don't have to recognize Red China just 'cause it happens to be the biggest country in the world, I shore as hell don't have to recognize Alaska just because it happens to be the biggest state in the Union."

In other words, Cousin Ed is a man with sharp logic, and you better stand out of the way unless you want some flint to fly in your eyes when he gets loose.

But I risked it anyway, and said, "Cousin Ed, what do you think of the right to dissent?"

"It's a sacred American right. One of the richest, finest American rights we've got and nobody better interfere with my right to dissent or I'll mash his face in for him.

"I'll tell you the thing that makes me sick at the stomach, though, is this here criticism.

"Criticize, criticize Lyndon—that's all these old critics can do. Why don't they leave Lyndon 'lone and let him fight his war in peace?

"If they want to criticize somebody, let them talk about that old billy-goat-faced thing called Ho Chi Minh. Why, that double-dyed old hypocrite stands up there and says, 'Get the foreigners out of Vietnam, get the foreigners out of Vietnam.' Johnny, I seen a picture of him and the crowd he runs with and they're the foreignest-looking outfits I ever laid eyes on.

"Not only that, Ho Chi Minh ain't got no consideration for us, but the critics don't jump on that. We go all the way over there at our own expense. We go there and try to fight a modern, up-to-date, civilized war, with tanks and flamethrowers and helicopters and bombers and napalm like the Lord intends people to use in this day and time. In broad daylight, too.

"And when do Ho Chi Minh and his crowd come out? After dark and on bicycles. Well, who in the world can fight with folks that are hateful like that?

"No, sir, I'll tell you this right now. I say this to these critics: if Ho Chi Minh and his crowd don't like what we're doing, let them go back where they come from.

"You know what's the matter with America? It's ignorance. Ignorance is what's ruining America today. Ain't nothing in the world that turns my stomach like these old ignorant doves. You can't teach them nothing. They won't learn nothing. I know, because I used to be in the same shape myself. I was ignorant. I didn't know what was happening. No matter how Dean Rusk would tell me, how Lyndon would tell me, I wouldn't listen. I enjoyed being ignorant.

"Then one day I heard a sermon by Billy Graham, and it opened my heart. And I heard a speech by Dean Rusk and it opened my mind. I decided I wasn't going to be ignorant on Vietnam. It was my civic duty to understand it. I went and got a geography book and looked it up. And let me tell you something. Right there is where the truth come to me in a blinding light. Vietnam ain't in Cuba! It's way the hell and gone over ten thousand miles off in a jungle. Now what does that tell us? It's a communist trick, ain't it. Communists will not start a war where it's convenient to fight them. Oh, they don't care about private enterprise. They don't care what it costs us to get over there. They don't care if every one of the taxpayers of America went broke. They'd just set there and laugh in your face.

"Let me tell you something else. It's also in Asia. Now what does that tell us about that place? Them Vietnamese is Asian foreigners. I don't know how many times I've heard smart people say an Asian foreigner is the most undependable type you can run into. You can't depend on them for shucks. Lyndon knows that. He has to bomb them. You can't depend on them to bomb theirselves.

"Why, we've been giving them guns and bullets for free over there for the last fifteen years. And not only that, we've been hauling the supplies to them at our own expense. They'd have laid their guns down and started working in rice paddies and singing songs long ago if we hadn't stayed right there and kept their minds on their business.

"Not only wouldn't them Vietnamese fight each other, but they wouldn't get out of the way and let *you* fight.

"I watch television and there'll be whole villages of them just standing there with their mouths open, and we have to go in with trucks and haul them all off and bulldoze the village to get on with our war. They couldn't care less. We've got I don't know how many thousand head of them penned up over there so's they'd be out of our way and we could get on with our war.

"But these old ignorant doves got to stand there and say 'Stop the bombing. You're killing civilians. You're killing civilians.'

"That ain't the reason we're over there. We're bombing them to win the hearts and minds of the people. If we accidentally kill somebody they make a big issue of it, you know. And I heard old Senator Fulbright say the other day, 'Old Ky and Thieu and that bunch, them South Vietnamese officials ain't nothing but military dictators.' So what if they are?

"These doves don't realize that we run through about forty of them South Vietnamese officials over there. We're down to the bottom of the barrel now. And if we didn't have Ky and Thieu, who would we have? You can't get choosy when you're narrowed down like that. Lyndon knows it, too.

"Just ask yourself this: if Jesus Christ was walking the Earth today and was over there in Vietnam, would our Savior be down there in them muddy rice paddies with a bunch of half-naked heathens? With people that wouldn't go to church if you invited them to services? People that don't even speak the English language.

"Or would He be up in those B52's and them Phantom bombers with them fine Christian boys who go to chapel and pray before each mission and know what they are doing with that napalm when they let go of it?"

Cousin Ed Snodgrass Explains China

"Do you know why I don't pay no mind to these old Vietnamese critics, Johnny? And why Dean Rusk don't pay no mind to them? Because we ain't worried about these old Vietnamese critics. Me and Dean Rusk is worried about just one thing in this world: China.

"He's the one that got me worried about it. I didn't understand it fully until Dean Rusk explained that thing to me. See, Dean Rusk is an authority on China. Yes, he's read a book on it and he understands what they're up to. He knows why we can't afford to recognize China.

"You know, you've heard every third person in the world is a Chinaman. I thought that was just propaganda.

"Well, I been all around Bastrop County and I never seen a Chinaman there. Seen a heap of colored and Mexicans, but no Chinamen. Fact, don't reckon I seen over five my whole life. You ask the average American citizen, 'How many Chinese have you seen a week?' And he'd have to tell you. 'Not over half a dozen at the outside.'

"Well, let me tell you something, that's the whole trick and Dean Rusk knows it. It's that way in America, but you get over there to Asia and it's another tune altogether.

"Oh yes, you know China is the biggest country over there: seven hundred million human beings. Not only are they Chinese—they're not ashamed of it. In fact, they're proud of it. They'll tell you right now, 'We was born Chinese and we're going to stay Chinese the rest of our life.' Shoot, they don't care how much it upsets Dean Rusk. No, he's on to them.

"You say, 'Well, if they've gone and got that numerous there in China, why don't we do what we're doing in Vietnam? Go in and thin them out.'

"Well, of course we can do that. But that ain't Dean Rusk's problem. See, he knows that old Mao Tse Tung runs that show in China. He's the old trickster, because Dean Rusk had documentary proof that Mao Tse Tung ain't nothing but an outright, un-American dues-paying communist.

"And Mao has it in for America and the free enterprise system here. That's what has got Dean Rusk so worried. He knows we could go into China like the Pentagon says and start a-bombing them. We could fight a war with China, with all its seven hundred million people, if they would fight fair and square. Dean Rusk knows that, too. He can figure. He's got paper and pencil.

"He knows that if we could bring our average up to what the military says we could, to killing a million Chinese a month, we'd have that war over and done with in maybe less than seventy-five years. If they would fight fair. Or if they would go back to an old Chinese custom they used to have called 'starving by the millions.' We could get it over and done with in maybe fifty years. Of course we can whip China. That ain't the question.

"But Mao Tse Tung has got a trick up them communist pajamas he wears. Oh, yes. He wants us to start a war with him some morning at ten o'clock. By the next day, twenty-four hours later, Mao would call Dean Rusk and say, 'We surrender. Come and count us, please.'

"Why, great goodness alive, do you know we would have to shut up every shop and close down every industry in America while every man, woman, and child in this country would have to go over there to start counting Chinamen? We'd spend the rest of our lives doing it. It would just wreck the private enterprise system in this country. And Mr. Mao Tse Tung knows it. Thank goodness Dean Rusk has his eye on them. He's doing the only intelligent thing people can do about China, and he knows it. Just don't recognize them and they'll give up after a while and go away."

VI
The Way the World Wags

VI

For many years, columns written by John Henry Faulk had a way of showing up in a variety of independent southern newspapers and journals, large and small. Some of these included the Petal (Mississippi) Paper, *the* Texas Observer, *the* Marble Falls (Texas) Highlander, *and the* Charlotte (North Carolina) News-Observer. *In the 1970s, Faulk's columns were syndicated by the* Los Angeles Times *and appeared all over the country. The columns gathered here date from 1973 and 1974, when the tides of Watergate were breaking on the American scene.*

Cowboy Dick's Last Ride

Here we are, ladies and gentlemen! Broadcasting to you live, directly from the arena at the Grand National Championship All-American Rodeo. The main event has just started! The event that has rodeo fans all over America on the edges of their seats. We are watching that Champ of Champions, that wild and woolly cowboy, the Amazing, Fantastic, Daring Dick Nixon come out of Chute Number One on the back of the orneryest, buckingest outlaw bronc in rodeo history—Watergate. It's a spectacular event—a duel between man and beast.

Daring Dick climbed into the saddle a moment ago with that self-assurance and calm confidence that have made him a champion rider. Daring Dick, as you know, long ago took the prize as the All-Time Champion trick rider. That's how he got his nickname, Tricky. Today, this isn't a trick ride; it's the real thing. The saddle-bronc ride. The big question is, will those many tricks Dick knows so well keep him in the saddle? Will he be able to stay on during this, the wildest, hardest ride of his career?

To catch you up, when they flung open the chute gate Watergate stood stock still and quivered. Daring Dick, sitting firmly in the saddle like he was riveted there, cut the bronc with his National Interest quirt. That did it! Ol' Watergate came out of the chute like a bolt of lightning, squalling, bucking, and headed straight up. Daring Dick dug his hand-forged National Security spurs in the bronc's shoulders and then in his flanks. Watergate hit the ground, hunched, then shot straight up again into the stars, pawing the air, snorting, and sunfishing. Fans swore they could see daylight between Daring Dick and the saddle. But Dick didn't come off. Ol' Watergate came pounding down, stiff-legged, and you could hear Daring Dick's grunt from the jolt.

Right now, Watergate's settled down to some of the roughest, meanest bucking ever seen in rodeo history. Daring Dick's lost his hat! If his head wasn't fastened on tight, it would come off, too. It's snapping backwards and forwards like a drum major's baton. Dick's hanging on for dear life! He's grasping that National Emergency saddle horn, with his teeth clenched and his eyes closed. He's making the ride of his life. Showing his fans that he's no quitter.

Ol' Watergate's no quitter, either. Daring Dick thought Watergate would be winded by now. But Watergate's proving his true breeding. His dam was Secrecy and his sire, Deceit. He's half-brother to Sabotage and full brother to Lying: all bad buckers and mean outlaws. Daring Dick wanted to bar Watergate from rodeo as too dangerous, but the fans would not allow it. Watching this ride, you can see why the champ would try to bar Watergate. That's the worst-bucking, bone-jolting bronco on the rodeo circuit! Ol' Watergate has already thrown a half-dozen of the best riders in the business.

To keep down the dust and to make the ride even more spectacular, the judges have spread impeachment all over the arena. When a rider is bucked off and hits that impeachment pavement, they have to carry him out. He can't get up and walk away.

Daring Dick must know that! Just look at that buckaroo hang on! Now his eyes are rolling wildly toward his pick-up men, Rebozo and Alplanalp. But they can't come to his aid. They are staying clear of Ol' Watergate's heels and teeth.

It's a mighty match between the champ rider and champ bronco! How long can the jolting, wrenching ride last? We'll have to watch and see. Right now, we'll pause for a commercial, with this reminder:

There never was a bronco that couldn't be rode.
There never was a cowboy who couldn't be throwed.

Nixon's Deposition

"If I was Dick Nixon right now," Cousin Ed Snodgrass declared yesterday, "you know what I'd do? I'd git up first thing tomorrow morning, I'd march myself down to the nearest courthouse there in Washington, I'd go before the judge, git myself swore, and here's what I'd aver and depose under oath:

"Your Honor, I want a writ of Habeas Corpus, a writ of Mandamus, a Cease and Desist order, an injunction, and any other of them legal things you might have on hand. I want to put a stop to all this caterwalling about me resigning or getting impeached. It's gitting on my nerves! Causing me to lose sleep, giving me stomach trouble, and interfering with my constitutional rights. It's also hurting my feelings.

"It's unfair, unconstitutional and violates my executive privilege plumb to hell and gone. I ain't going to put up with it! I want this court to order it stopped today!

"Just look at what they are complaining about! They say I lied to the American people about Watergate! Well, what if I did? Back in 1968, I promised the American people that I'd stop the war in Vietnam, if they would elect me president. They elected me. Instead of stopping that war, I spread it out all over Southeast Asia. Into Laos and Cambodia. I bombed harder and more than ever. In 1972 I still had that war going. So every voter in the country knowed I lied to them back in 1968, when I told them I'd stop it. Yet, they elected me for four more years! Now they're bad-mouthing me because of a few little lies about Watergate! Your Honor, that's what I call swallowing a camel and straining on a gnat! It's plumb hypocritical!

"And if the court please, I just wish you would look at what else they are charging! They claimed I used dirty tricks in my election in 1972. Why, so I did! But I'd been using those same shady tricks ever since I first ran for office back in 1946. Ask my first opponent, Jerry Voorhees, or my second one, Helen Gehagen Douglas. Or ask the Democrats if I didn't call them a party of traitors back in the fifties. Why, I was known by the name Tricky Dicky. Yet them same Democrats founded the Democrats for Nixon in 1972, deserted their party by the millions to vote for me.

"They are barking and baying now that I'm the buggingest, wiretappingest president ever. Why, me and Spiro spent three years before 1972 preaching the gospel of wiretapping. Claimed I had an inherent right to wiretap as I pleased. Ever' one of those millions of Americans that voted for me last year knew that fact. Same with their claiming now that I'm against free speech and a free press. I sure am. Always have been. And I said it loud and often all during my first term. Lambasted protesters as bums and tore into the press as biased and sinful. I never hid my feelings under no bushel when it come to free speech and free press. Yet, the voters flocked to the polls last year to reelect me. And 95 percent of the newspapers in this country supported me.

"Your Honor, I'm exactly the same Richard Nixon today that I was last year. My principles and policies is exactly the same today that they was last year. I never ran as no brand-new strange politician last year. Everything about me and the way I operate was knowed to the American people before they reelected me, including Watergate. Remember, I asked for four more years on my public record. I maintain that now, if they are faulting me for a few lies I told about Watergate, after approving the big ones I told them about the war and bombing and all, they are all hypocrites. I also maintain that if the American people endorsed my principles and policies by that big vote last year, it's likely whoever they would get to replace me wouldn't be much different.

"So if the Court please, I want a Cease and Desist order issued against that crowd that's trying to impeach me. And I want it right now. Today! If it took them twenty-five years to catch on to me, they ought to have to put up with me for another three years. By the way, Your Honor, I want an injunction against Barry Goldwater while I'm at it. Last week he stated that my credibility is zero. Me and Barry's been good friends, fed from the same trough, for a quarter of a century. I maintain that if it took him twenty-five years to find out that my credibility was zero, he ought to be made to keep his mouth shut about it now."

Defending National Security

At last I understand what national security means. That is, what it means to Cousin Ed Snodgrass and his friends. He explained it to me the other morning about daylight when he came over to have a cup of coffee with me.

"Got a letter from Senator John Tower's office yesterday," he remarked as he blew on his coffee. "Really was an eye-opener, too. Tower understands the whole thing!"

"What whole thing does Senator Tower understand?" I asked.

"All this plotting and conspiring against our national security," he answered. "Tower's on to the whole shooting match. Them conspirators ain't got John Tower fooled for one minute."

"What conspirators are you talking about, Cousin Ed?"

"Sam Ervin and his committee, the *New York Times*, *Washington Post*, and them high and mighty TV commentators that's plotting against national security. That's what conspirators I'm talking about!"

"What kind of conspiracy are they in against national security?"

"They are conspiring to git Dick Nixon!"

"Did Senator Tower say that the Watergate investigations were a conspiracy against national security?"

"No. He just pointed out that they were all so prejudiced and one-sided that it amounted to a conspiracy to git President Nixon. I figured out the rest for myself."

"You know, Cousin Ed, you and Senator Tower and your friends amaze me. In fact, you dumbfound me. Here we are a self-governing people, a society that boasts about the fact that we control our government and that it does not control us. Teach our children that. Then we discover that the men whom we have entrusted with power have lied to us and deceived us. And right off, you raise the howl that it's unfair to investigate the wrongdoing! You even call it a conspiracy."

"Now wait a minute! Me and Senator Tower ain't defending no wrongdoing. We believe everybody that's done wrong ought to be punished. We just say leave President Nixon's name out of it."

"But he's head of the administration that's perpetrated all the wrongdoing and deception that caused such a crisis! How do you think they can leave his name out?"

"They ain't proved a thing on Nixon yet! He's pure as the driven snow. That's why it's so unfair to go 'round accusin' him."

"Hogwash, Cousin Ed. What do you want them to prove? His own aides, members of his administration have publicly confessed to perjury, obstruction of justice, burglary, and God knows what other crimes. His own staff now admit that he instructed them to follow a 'basic policy decision' to keep secret the gross misuses of the taxpayers' money to the tune of ten million dollars on Nixon's private homes. That's not speculation. That's now admitted fact. Add to those things the fact that last week the Pentagon itself was forced to admit that it had systematically falsified records of bombing in Cambodia in order to deceive the American people. At whose instruction? Nixon's! And you sit there and say the Senate committee and newspapers are unfair to President Nixon. What nonsense."

"I said, and I repeat, I ain't defending no wrongdoing. I'm defending our national security."

"Then why are you claiming that the investigators are all conspiring in a plot against national security? Our national security isn't dependent on official misconduct. To the contrary, lying and deception threaten our nation's well-being."

"Son, anything that threatens Dick Nixon threatens our national security. That's just a matter of common sense."

"What's common sense about that?"

"If you was smart as me and Senator Tower, you'd know! Dick Nixon *is* national security. Anybody that goes around criticizing Dick Nixon is undermining our national security. If you don't believe me, ask the president."

Making an Honest Living

"Honest man can't make a living in this country no more!" Mr. Hub Todsy told me the other day. "It's all over! My best friend's let me down. I'm closing shop. Let subversion take over."

"What's happened now, Mr. Todsy?" I asked.

"Nixon's done went and invited that feller Brezhnev over here. Had him cavorting all over Washington, swiggin' champagne, dancing jigs in front of TV, and making hisself at home. It's the end of the line for me," he said sadly.

"You objected to Brezhnev's visit? Why?"

" 'Course I did! Don't you know who Brezhnev is? He just happens to be a full-blooded un-American subversive! Got a procommunist record a mile long!"

"Everybody knows Brezhnev is the secretary general of the Communist Party of Russia, Mr. Todsy. But what has that got to do with you making an honest living?"

"It's got a hell of a lot to do with me making a living in my line of business! It's shot me plumb out of the saddle."

"How? I thought you were a plumber."

"Naw! That's only a front. I run a reporting and informing business. Report subversives, un-Americans, and that sort of thing."

"Well, it looks like you would be doing a landslide business these days, what with all those Russian reporters, officials, and diplomats that Brezhnev brought along with him. They were all over the place."

"You don't understand, son," Mr. Todsy shook his head. "I don't report Russian subversives. No call for them sort. I just report American subversives. And now, Dick Nixon's let me down and I'm as good as out of business."

"How has President Nixon let you down?"

"It's this way. Back yonder when him and Joe McCarthy had the Democrats ducking and dodging from them treason charges; back when hating reds was patriotic Americanism, Dick Nixon inspired me to go into business! Me and my wife set up a business called 'Committee to Combat the Communist Takeover in Texas.' We took down the names of everybody we caught trying to overthrow Texas—schoolteachers, preachers, college professors, everybody. We got bankers and businessmen to sponsor us. We worked with the FBI, the House Un-American Activities Committee, the American Legion, the Texans for America—all them patriotic groups. Anytime they needed inside information on who was subversive, who was un-American, or even un-Texan, we was right there with the last word on the subject. It was wonderful. We never got rich, but we made a good living. 'Course, we had to work at it, stay on the job, but we didn't mind. We was appreciated for it. J. Edgar Hoover sent us a letter praising our good work. The American Legion give us a plaque for our patriotism. We was invited to speak before civic clubs and patriotic organizations all over Texas. Them was the days."

"What did you speak on, Mr. Todsy?" I asked, as he paused and smiled nostalgically.

"Oh, on about the same thing Dick Nixon talked about in them days, 'cept we just talked about how the reds was taking over Texas, and he talked on how they was fixing to overthrow the U.S.A."

"And now you feel like your business is doomed?"

"No doubt about it. For the last several years, business had been slipping. Got to where folks didn't scare as easy as they used to. A few chambers of commerces and the American Legion still called on us for information. But not so often as before. Now that Dick Nixon's took to inviting them genuine red Russians over here, pumping their hands and huggin' 'em in public, I'm throwing in the towel."

"Do you resent President Nixon for that?"

"Well, no. But I'll say this: Dick Nixon put me in business; and he's put me out of business."

Nixon's Tree

"Told you they'd never tree Dick Nixon! For good, that is," Cousin Ed Snodgrass crowed as he sat down in the kitchen to have coffee with me last Friday morning about daylight. "Nawsir! They might tree him. But Dick won't stay treed. He's too slick for 'em."

"Seems to me Nixon's about to run out of trees to hide in, Cousin Ed," I commented as I poured him a cup of coffee.

"Well, he ain't! If you wasn't so closed-minded you'd know he's too foxy to stay treed. Why, last summer when he made that there categorical denial, you thought they had him. Then he jumped and run behind that 'executive privilege.' They flushed him out of there and he got up that 'I'm responsible, but my hired hands are to blame' tree. You and them newsmen and senators might think he's gonna stay up that tree. But he's done give you the slip. He's done off and runnin' agin."

"How do you know?"

"Seen him last night on TV! He pulled his POW's on 'em. It was plumb inspirin'."

"What do you mean 'he pulled his POW's on 'em'?"

"Didn't you watch that there POW party Dick give there at the White House?"

"I didn't see it. But what's that got to do with his Watergate trouble?"

"Good Lord, son, where was you when they passed out gumption? Don't you know that next to motherhood and the flag, there ain't no more potent political club a man can lay hands on these days than the POW's? It's outright dynamite. And Dick was workin' it for all it was worth last night."

"Yeah. But your friend Nixon has about worn that POW business threadbare. He can't get much more mileage out of the POW's."

"There you go! Underestimating Dick agin! You just ought to of seen Dick and his POW's last night. Put the big pot in the little one! Abso-damn-lutely splendid! A million flags a wavin', all red, white, and blue. Spankin' color guards a-marchin'. Bands a-playin'. Everybody salutin' everybody else. Dick toastin' the POW's. The POW's toastin' Dick. Both of 'em toastin' their wives. Bob Hope and John Wayne a-hurrahin' for Old Glory. Dick a-tellin' how much he loved America and his POW's. POW's tellin' how much they love America and Dick. Nobody was even thinkin' Watergate, let alone mentionin' it! It was all so glorious and beautiful! Thought I was goin' to have to git my tinted specs to watch it, it was so dazzling!"

"Yes, but what about the thousands of crippled and maimed veterans lying in hospitals around the country? And the families of soldiers who were killed? And the thousands of unemployed veterans and their families? You think they were all that dazzled as they watched it?"

"I don't know. But that ain't the point. The point is, Dick ain't about to stay treed. He proved it last night."

"You think he can duck behind that POW issue every time they tree him?"

"No sir! Dick's done got his real hidin' place picked out. Told the POW's about it yesterday."

"What's his real hiding place?"

"National security! Said yesterday 'I'm going to protect the national security of the United States as far as our secrets are concerned.' You watch! They'll never flush him out, long as he's behind that national security. It works like a charm."

"Cousin Ed, you're just as wrong as Nixon is if you think the American people are that gullible. They're not going to let the crimes and corruption of Nixon's administration be buried under any 'nation security' humbug."

"Think not? Well, you just wait till Dick wraps hisself up in red, white, and blue, marches out, and fires that national security cannon at that Senate Watergate Committee. You'll see 'em take to their heels. Dick won't be treed. His critics will be the ones that's treed."

"That's where you're wrong. And Nixon's wrong. He thinks he can manipulate the American people with patriotic slogans forever and they'll never catch on. That's not so."

"Son, Dick Nixon can handle patriotism like Lindbergh handled an airplane. And don't you forget it."

"That might be so. But what if the American people decide in this case that Sam Johnson was right when he observed, 'Patriotism is the last refuge of a scoundrel'?"

"Might be the last refuge of a scoundrel. But it's also a safe refuge."

Quick Dick

"Dick Nixon has done won," Cousin Ed Snodgrass declared the other day when I stopped by his place for a visit. "Yessir! Dick is too slick and too quick for you boys. You ain't going to corner him. You might as well give up trying."

"If you're talking about his latest big speech when he turned over those transcripts, Cousin Ed," I replied, "you're wrong. As J. R. Parten says, that speech wouldn't fool a right young turkey."

"Dick never made that speech to turkeys. Made it to people— the people of this country. And he never turnt loose them transcripts to no turkeys. Turnt them loose to people. He went to the people with his evidence."

"Evidence! Why Cousin Ed, you know those transcripts are not evidence! They are nothing more than a carefully edited, pruned version of what went on between Nixon and his aides. Not the full account at all. The Judiciary Committee won't let him get away with that piece of transparent trickery. He hasn't won this round yet."

"Hold on a minute, son! Have you read them transcripts?"

"I've read portions of them. And I've heard other portions of them read over television. I'll say this. They are pretty shocking."

"That's right! Even being a bobtailed version, as you say, they got some pretty rough stuff in them, ain't they?"

"Sure do. Why, in places it sounds like a pack of gangsters. Nixon, Haldeman, and Erhlichman discussing how to use national security as a cover for their rascalities. Dean and Nixon discussing how to make payoffs; which alibis will work. It's enough to turn a man's stomach to read about such shoddy dealings in the White House!"

"Oh its plumb shocking, ain't it!" Cousin Ed mocked.

"Yes, dammit, it is!"

"But shenanigans and double-dealing ain't the point!" he shot back. "You and your Nixon critics are so anxious to pick out them little piddling things, you've missed the real point of them tapes, what Dick keeps saying over and over again, all through them talks. You missed what Dick is really all about. That's why he's got you beat. Beat hands down."

"What are you talking about, Cousin Ed?"

"All through them conversations, Dick keeps repeating, 'the people don't care. It's just our critics we have to worry about. The people of this country don't give a damn about Watergate. They'd like to forget it.' Remember how often he repeats that?"

"Yes, I do! And that's one of the most disgraceful things about the shoddy business. It shows a contempt for the people of this country."

"No such of a thing! It shows Dick knows what he's talking about!"

"You mean that the American people don't care how immoral and cynical their leaders are? I'm ashamed of you, Cousin Ed!"

"Ain't got a thing to do with morals and ethics! It's got to do with responsibility. All in the world Dick Nixon is saying is that the people don't want to be bothered with the responsibility of government. They've let the government do their thinking for them so long, now they don't care. He's saying that because he believes it. He believes it and he's betting on it!"

"Well, he's making a mighty risky bet, Cousin Ed. He's just liable to find out that the people feel a lot more responsible than he figured."

"You and your friends go ahead and believe that! Go ahead! But don't try to git me and Dick Nixon to swaller it. Nosir! Not 'til you can come up with more proof of it than has been showed in any election in the last twenty years. Dick's winning out because he knows people like to be told everything's going to be all right, not given the responsibility for *making* everything come out right. It's just that simple. Dick knows it. He's done won."

Wading into Watergate

"If Congress is so everlasting anxious to impeach somebody, let it impeach itself!" Cousin Ed Snodgrass snorted the other morning when I went by his place to have coffee with him.

"I guess you're trying to say you're against that impeachment move that's going on in Congress now," I said.

"I ain't trying to say no such thing," he snapped indignantly. "I'm saying that if they got the grounds, let them go ahead and impeach Nixon. That's just fine and dandy. But at the same time they ought to do the fair and honest thing and impeach themselves."

"What's Congress done now to rile you up so, Cousin Ed?"

"Congress has now did just what it's been doing for the last ten years—Nothing! Abso-flat-lutely nothing!"

"Why it certainly has! Congress has hopped to and started the impeachment proceedings! That's a pretty history-making move!"

"Well, I would remind you that impeaching presidents ain't the only line of business that Congress is s'pose' to be in. It's got a raft of duties besides that one. It's what it ain't doing about its other duties that's plumb disgraceful."

"Be specific, Cousin Ed."

"Durn tootin' I'll be specific! Congress ain't done nothing in the last ten years but roll over and play dead ever' time a real issue looked it in the eye. And I don't see no evidence that it aims to change its ways. Look at all the things Watergate has turnt up! What's Congress doing about them?"

"Things like what?"

"Things like the shoddy campaign spending; millions of dollars poured out to elect special-interest candidates; everybody knows it's a sin and a shame. Has Congress done a single thing about it? Nosir! Things like reforming the practices that brought on Watergate. Congress made a move? Nawsir!

"Or for that matter, what's it done about its own wore-out, good-for-nothing seniority system that allows some of the most incompetent political hacks in Congress to sit in charge of its most important committees, bottling up and blocking any legislation that don't meet their personal approval? Congress done a thing about that? Or unfair tax laws that's letting the real rich and the big corporations ride free, while the ordinary citizens get gouged. Congress moved on that? Nawsir! You name the issue, and I guarantee you I'll tell you what Congress ain't done about it."

"Now don't forget, Cousin Ed, Nixon has vetoed a lot that Congress has done in the last five years."

"Don't try to dose me with that old stale medicine! This country might have a Republican president, but it's got a Democratic Congress. Congress can't git away with blaming it all on Nixon. Them congressmen been playing possum too long."

"Well, maybe this year the Democrats are going to take control and really get on the ball."

"Them Democrats that's done in Congress are all sitting around waiting for some plums to fall in their laps next November. But I maintain they ain't done nothing to deserve the plums. I don't mind faulting Nixon for his shortcomings. But Congress ain't got nothing to brag about right now."

"Cousin Ed, with inflation eating up the people's incomes, with hard times riding their way, and with confidence in public officials at an all-time low, don't you think there's a pretty good chance that Congress will be forced to get moving on some of these problems?"

"I ain't going to hold my breath waiting for that to happen, son. Congress reminds me of an old, overfed steer that's walked off into the mud around a waterhole and got bogged down to his belly. He makes a few grunts and moves to git out, then sort of settles down, too trifling to figure out what to do next. Take a team of mules and a cattle prod to budge 'im."

"That seems to be a little rough on Congress, Cousin Ed. After all, most congressmen are anxious to hold their jobs. So they try to reflect what their constituents want. In that respect, it's actually the fault of the voters if Congress fails to do its duty."

"Oh no! That ol' dog won't hunt! If I ask you for a job, and you hire me to look after your business, and I promise to do it, then

I let your business go to rack and ruin, you ain't going to let me git by with saying it was your fault for hiring me."

"You've got a good point there, Cousin Ed."

"That's my whole point! I maintain we ought to take a good look at the whole picture right now. Just because Dick Nixon has waded off into Watergate, floundered, and is about to git hisself impeached, ain't no reason for us to allow Congress to roll its eyes towards heaven and act pious and self-righteous when it ain't been picking up its end of the load. Just because you're mad at a man for selling you moldy cornmeal, ain't no reason to excuse his pardner for selling you rotten potatoes."

Hypocrites and Bootleggers

"Yessir! When it comes to genuine, rock-ribbed, fourteen-carat hypocrisy," Cousin Ed Snodgrass began yesterday morning as we sat drinking coffee in my kitchen, "give me the news media of this country. You newspaper boys reminds me of a bunch of bootleggers peddling whiskey all week then coming to church on Sunday and testifying against the evils of drink."

"What brought that on, Cousin Ed?" I asked.

"Been reading about how you news fellers has been rolling your eyes and clucking your tongues over Dick Nixon's enemy lists. Just shocked you to your toes. Didn't it? Can't believe such a thing could happen! My, my, my . . . Durn hypocrites!"

"What's hypocritical about being shocked at Nixon's enemy list? Pretty shoddy business, if you ask me."

"Ain't it though! Just outrageous! Scandalous! Why? I'll tell you why! 'Cause Dick Nixon done it! That's why! Oh yes, we know they been putting out enemy lists for the last twenty-five years. But that's not shocking. Fact, not even worth mentioning. We're just outraged and upset cause Dick Nixon done it! Why, it's enough to turn a man's stomach, such two-faced prejudice!"

"You don't know what you're talking about, Cousin Ed. No other administration, Democratic or Republican, ever compiled an enemy list to harass its opponents. You know it!"

"If you had some brains, instead of a head full of prejudice, you would know they was putting out political enemy lists before Dick Nixon ever come near the White House. Ever since ol' Harry Truman was mismanaging the country."

"You're talking through your hat, Cousin Ed. Since Harry Truman's administration? You can't prove that!"

"Can and will! Back yonder under Truman, Congress set up that House Un-American Committee. One of its biggest jobs was running off lists of names of citizens it decided was enemies. Political enemies. Newspapers hurrahed and throwed their hats in the air. It was all great patriotic work. Congress would make the lists and the newspapers would headline them. Drive people out of work, ruin their reputations. That was all just fine. Before long Truman put his attorney general into the enemy listing business. Didn't charge them with no crime; didn't give them no trial in court. Just listed them as enemies."

"Hold on, Cousin Ed! Those lists were different from the enemy list Nixon worked up."

"Nope. Just the same. Political enemies: citizens with wrong politics. Only difference was the folks on them other enemy lists usually lost their jobs and got disgraced. Far as I know, that ain't happened to nobody on Dick's enemy list."

"And a lot of responsible citizens objected to all that listing business, too."

"If they did, they kept mighty quiet about it, or else they ended up on a list too! And one thing sure! Every congressman and president since Truman backed up the operation or kept their mouths shut! Got to where every outfit in the country was keeping lists of political enemies; American Legion, all them sort of outfits, and the almighty free press was baying along after them enemies like a pack of potlikker hounds after a stray cat! Enemy lists was just jim-dandy then. But you let Dick Nixon get one up, and all hell breaks loose!"

"You're all confused, Cousin Ed. The country had gone hysterical over subversives. Those lists were made up by official government agencies. It was a sorry period. But, at least it had an official sanction."

"Why, hell, what's more official than the official president of the United States? Sure, people on them so-called official lists was subversives. But who said so? Some official in Washington! They was also American citizens who hadn't committed no crime nor broke no law. But they was harassed and tormented just the same. Punished for their politics. Teachers, preachers, movie actors— anybody and everybody that had the wrong sort of politics was put on the enemies list! Well, Nixon put folks on his list that had the wrong sort of politics from his point of view."

"Yes, but nothing in the Constitution, which Nixon swore to uphold, gives him the right to use the power of his office to punish his political opponents."

"And nothing in that there same Constitution that every official in this country, from congressman down to county commissioner swears to uphold, gives any government official, the FBI, the American Legion, or anybody else the right to harass and shut up their political opponents. But they all did it! And some are still trying it. But what kind of hell-raising do you hear from you smart alecks in the press? Nothin'! You throw a conniption fit when Dick Nixon puts the editor of the *New York Times* on his enemy list. You was all-fired quiet — and so was the *New York Times* — when a congressional committee put the editor of some little left-wing paper on its list.

"Dick Nixon might shade the truth sometimes. He might even be a little over-pious sometimes. But when it comes to bald-faced, out-and-out, double-standard hypocrisy, Dick Nixon can't trot in harness 'long side the newspaper fellers."

Snodgrass on Reagan

Cousin Ed Snodgrass was in fine fettle. I could tell it at once when I stopped by his place to have coffee with him the other morning. His step had an extra spring, his eye an extra sparkle.

"You're acting mighty spry this morning, Cousin Ed," I commented as he poured me a cup of coffee.

"Feeling prime! Plumb prime," he replied. "Man's got to git up and go in this world. Can't sit around and study his troubles all the time. Got to have foresight! Look ahead!"

"Tell me what's happened, Cousin Ed. Don't keep me in suspense."

"Nothing's happened. Nothing at all! Except that I've got me a man that can save this country! While you smart-aleck, know-it-all liberals have been licking your chops and closing in on Dick Nixon, I've got out and rustled me a feller that can step in and save this country from your schemes to take over. Man that can head you off and hold the fort."

"You think Gerald Ford's the answer to your prayers, Cousin Ed?"

"Ain't talking 'bout Ford! He's a good man, but I got sense enough to know you birds would tear him to pieces for getting picked by Dick. I know you. Know your underhanded ways. Nothing you'd love better than to get after Ford with that 'He was Dick's choice'!"

"The only other person I ever heard you go all out for is John Connally. You think John's the man for '76?"

"Was. But not now. Don't you think I've got sense enough to know John Connally's milk business has gone sour on him?"

"Then who is it, for goodness sakes?"

"If you and your crowd could stop wallering around in Watergate for a minute and think about this country's welfare for a change, you would know. It's the perfect candidate: Ronald Reagan!"

"Ronnie Reagan! Good Lord, Cousin Ed, Reagan's to the right of General Walker! Why even *Goldwater* looks like a New Dealer upside Reagan."

"Well what about it?"

"Why, you seem to think that the voters of this country haven't learned anything in the last two years! With inflation, unemployment, and Watergate, the people of this country are not going to fall for Reagan and his simplistic, right-wing guff."

"You boys think you're all-fired smart, don't you? You think just because you've syphoned off all Dick Nixon's credibility and leaked it out on the ground, you've stopped the bus. Well, you ain't! Sure you've undid the best president this country ever had. But you ain't in the driver's seat yet. And what's more, you ain't ever going to be. Ronald Reagan is going to take over."

"O.K. Tell me why you're so sure."

"First place, it ain't got nothing to do with his politics. It's got to do with his training. He's trained up for the job. Went about it with foresight, looking ahead."

"What are you talking about! Reagan was a movie actor—a professional actor—before he got into politics. He hadn't any political training at all!"

"Got you there! That's exactly why he is so strong! Look at Spiro Agnew. Wonderful actor! When he come down on the effete snobs and protestors; when he spoke out for law and order, he rocked his audience from coast to coast. But he wasn't a good enough actor to carry it off when they started heckling him with felony charges. Got run off the stage."

"That's an understatement!"

"Same with Dick Nixon. Wonderful actor too. Really had folks convinced. But he wasn't no professional at the business. Had the shortcoming of looking guilty even when he was innocent. But what have you got with Ronald Reagan? Everything in one!"

"Meaning what?"

"Meaning that he's the real article. He studied acting. Made it his line of business before he ever fooled with politics. Learnt it from the bottom up. Now he can handle anything that comes down the pike."

"You really think so, Cousin Ed?"

"I'm certain so! Take Spiro. When he said he wasn't no extortionist, he wasn't actor enough to make folks believe him. When Dick said 'I'm not a crook,' he wasn't actor enough to be convincing. But you let somebody call Reagan a horse thief and see what happens!"

"What will happen?"

"Reagan will look them in the eye, fair and square, and say 'I raise horses, I don't have to steal them! Next question!' Reagan's a professional actor. No politician is right all the time. But he's got to be a good enough actor to make folks believe that he is. That's where Reagan shines."

The Game's the Same

"Let's git on with the game!" Cousin Ed allowed happily the other morning. "Got a brand new dealer in the dealer's seat! Name of Gerald Ford. Let's git to playing again and see what sort of cards he deals."

"You sure didn't spend much time mourning for your friend Dick Nixon, Cousin Ed. Poor man's down and out, and here you are whooping it up for Ford already."

"Son, Dick might be out. But Dick ain't down," he announced. "Dick left office like he left Vietnam—with honor!"

"Cousin Ed, why are you so hardheaded! Dick Nixon left office in disgrace. He might not admit it. And you might not admit it. But it's a fact."

"Tommyrot!" Cousin Ed snorted. "You heared his farewell speech! Did he sound disgraced? You heared what Ford said right after he resigned? Said Dick had made the greatest personal sacrifice a man ever made for his country! And every single big Republican in Washington along with blame near all the Democrats got up and give out with the same sentiments! And you sitting there going on 'bout disgrace!"

"Maybe they just wanted to make sure he left," I countered.

"Nawsir! I maintain when a man has half the town out waving goodbye to him, while he climbs into Air Force One and goes sailing out to his million-dollar estate in California—that ain't leaving in disgrace. That's leaving in high style."

"The fact remains, Cousin Ed, that Dick Nixon has a grim future ahead of him."

"Sure wish to God my future was that grim," Cousin Ed nodded. "Strolling around a million-dollar estate, with a $60,000-a-year pension guaranteed for life, a $96,000-a-year expense account, and goodness knows what other privileges—all for free. It's just plumb pitiful, ain't it?"

"I'm not talking about that, Cousin Ed, and you know it! I'm talking about the cruel, hard realities that he has to live with the rest of his life."

"Like what?"

"Like the fact that he is the only president in the history of this country ever to be named an unindicted coconspirator by a grand jury; like the fact that he's the only president ever to be run out of office charged with lying to Congress and the American people, obstruction of justice, and other crimes; like the fact that he chose a vice-president who was a practicing felon, and in addition has had a couple dozen of his top aides, as well as our former cabinet members, indicted for felonies. That's a pretty hideous record for a man to have to live with."

"Shore it is," Cousin Ed came back. "If a man thought about it like that. But Dick don't. Dick goes to bed in that fine big bed of his every night with the happy thought that for the rest of his life he can say, 'I'm the only man in the history of this country who ever had the honor and privilege of personally and by myself picking out a president for the United States'!"

"He might not be sleeping in that big bed always, Cousin Ed. Remember he's Citizen Nixon now, not President Nixon. He's not immune from prosecution any more."

"Now you are talking through your hat," Cousin Ed said. "Why, Dick Nixon knows there ain't a chance in the world that he'll ever come to trial."

"What makes you so sure of that?"

"Something that you are plumb short on," Cousin Ed declared. "Common sense! You had any common sense, you'd know that by the time they git through trying all those aides and former associates of Dick's, they'll use up every potential juror in the country. Won't be twelve people left to pick for a jury. 'Course that ain't the only reason."

"That's a fool reason, Cousin Ed. What are the other reasons you think he won't get tried?"

"Well, there's the fact that Dick's friends won't allow it. He's still a hero to the law and order folks."

"But he has publicly admitted that he lied!" I protested. "And the Judiciary Committee has documented his crimes!"

"Right there's one of the peculiarities of America, son. Them double-standard folks! Ones that barked the loudest 'bout law and order and lack of morals in America is the exact same crowd that will be howling the loudest for leniency for Dick. That's why I say Dick ain't down, he's just out."

"And so you think that's the reason Nixon won't have to face any criminal charges?"

"No! The main reason he won't is that the boys in Washington want to git the game started again. They've got Ford in the dealer's chair, they're ready to get to playing their game. Ain't got time to bother with Dick no more. He's out!"

"Not so fast, Cousin Ed. It was not just the dealer that was messing up the game, as you call it. Some of the rules they've been using were out of kilter, too. A lot of thoughtful people want some of those slippery rules changed."

He looked at me and shook his head. "Son," he said solemnly, "out there in Nevada, when the boys that run them big casinos find out that one of their dealers has been caught cheating, they run him off and git a new dealer. But they don't change the rules of their game. Oh no! Not when they've been winning with them rules! Might talk like they're going to give the public a better break. But they don't. If you think them power boys in Washington plays different, you're crazy. They've changed dealers. The game's the same."

Law and Order

Mr. Jaworski is getting all sorts of advice on what he ought to do with/to/about Dick Nixon now that Dick's been pried loose from that executive privilege. It seems everybody in Washington has an opinion on the matter, but the opinions are different. That places Mr. Jaworski in a mischief of a dilemma, sitting there with four or five boxcars full of painfully researched evidence and not knowing where to deliver it.

By great good luck, my friend Peavine Jeffries, down in North Zulch, Texas, put his mind to the matter and has come up with an equitable, fair solution for Mr. Jaworski. One that just about everybody, including Dick Nixon, can agree is reasonable all the way around.

Peavine explained his proposal to me yesterday. "Johnny, I reckon you've noticed that while inflation is the number one problem in America, it ain't the one that's gittin' the most attention right now. Nawsir, the one that's causing the most talk and confusion is what's the fair thing to do about Dick Nixon and all them crimes he allegedly committed.

"Republikins is all asweat to put as much distance between theirselves and Watergate as they can by November. So they keep sending up trial balloons—like all the sudden coming out for amnesty for our war resisters and hinting that Dick's done suffered enough; or now that he's been hung, he oughtn't be drawed and quartered. In other words, they want to git Mr. Jaworski to call off his dogs and forget the whole thing. That don't make no sense much, since the Republikins in Congress was the exact ones that went and caused Dick to resign because he'd played a fast one on them with that confession of his that he'd obstructed justice. They don't cut much mustard with that 'We decided he was guilty, but we wish you'd think of him as innocent.'

"Democrats is so busy buttin' heads with each other that they can't take time out to advise Mr. Jaworski one way or the other. Or maybe it's just that they got gratitude and feel kindly towards Dick Nixon. He made them look better than they've managed to make theirselves look here lately.

"So what have we got? Confusion all over the place. But the answer has been right there all along! They've just muddied up the water and confused Mr. Jaworski so he ain't been able to think it out.

"Last night I was playing dominoes with three of my friends. They had three different opinions on how the Dick Nixon business ought to be handled. Ranged all the way from throwing the book at him to letting him go without even putting the evidence of his so-called crimes before the grand jury.

"Well sir, I went to bed thinking about it last night and woke up this morning with it still on my mind. All the sudden, before breakfast, mind you, the truth come to me in a blinding light. There was only one sure-fire way to decide what to do! And here it is:

"Now what's causing all the confusion? Why, the fact that we've got a prominent citizen, a man that has held the highest office in the land, suspected of some felony crimes. But, he's so prominent and held such a respected office, that we don't know whether he even ought to be indicted, let alone made to stand trial. More than that, it's going to hurt a lot of people's feelings if he is put through the wringer. It's going to hurt a lot of folks' feelings if he ain't.

"So how do you figure out what's the best thing to do? The right and proper course to follow? Why, for something that important, you get out and find the best authority on the subject in the land. That's what you do!

"It just so happens that we've got just such an authority in this country right now. An authority on law and order, how to deal with lawbreakers and their punishment. An authority who has thought and spoken more on the subject than any man in history. He said almost everything there was to be said on the subject. Many, many times.

"And best of all, you don't have to go out and hunt up the authority. You can read his thoughts and speeches on the subject, 'cause he left them for all to see! Starting in 1968, when he pointed out that the Democrats had been slack on law enforcement and caused a crime wave, every month or so he lectured in detail on what a terrible thing it is to coddle criminals and wink at crime; for soft-headed judges to let criminals off with light sentences; how terrible the thought of amnesty is; and most of all, how each man must be held responsible for the crimes he commits.

"That's the authority who ought to be consulted. Won't have to look him up, even. Just consult what he's said over the past five years on law enforcement and criminal justice, and Mr. Jaworski will know exactly what to do with Dick Nixon."

Amnesty International

Mr. Gerald Ford, President
The White House
Washington, D.C.

Dear President Ford:

Would you please settle an argument between me and my neighbor,

Jim Snorles? We've been going around and around on it for the past week. Now, we've agreed to accept your word on the matter.

A couple of weeks ago, at your news conference, you answered several questions about the CIA's plotting against the constitutionally elected government of a sovereign state, Chile. You said that you thought that it was just Jim Dandy for agents of the United States to sneak in and sabotage a democratically elected government, and implied that if our plotting and planning resulted in a bloody military dictatorship, such as happened in the case of Chile, that was O.K. too. You even made a statement to the effect that there was nothing wrong with Henry Kissinger and the 40 Committee, through the CIA, arbitrarily and secretly committing the government of the United States to such a lawless policy and then lying under oath to the American people about it.

In sum, your statements added up to a public commitment to international piracy and lawlessness. No president of the United States in all our history ever publicly took such a stand before. No head of state, in fact, in our memory, except Adolph Hitler, ever proclaimed such a policy for his nation. Since your thinking and politics in no way resemble those of Hitler, my friend Snorles and I are in great dispute as to why you proclaimed the law of the jungle to be part and parcel of this country's foreign policy.

I argue that it was because you thought you were standing on your feet and accidently put them both in your mouth at the same time. Snorles says it's because Lyndon Johnson was right about you playing too much football bareheaded. Which one of us is right?

> Yours sincerely,
> John Faulk

P.S. My friend Snorles is thinking about robbing a bank. What is your policy on that? Should he arrange for a pardon before he commits the crime or after he is caught?

Ford's Ace

"Republicans might have lost a hand at the polls," Cousin Ed Snodgrass declared this morning as we sat having coffee, "but President Ford's still holding a big ace. He'll take the pot in this game."

"What big ace is President Ford holding, Cousin Ed?"

"That there WIN program of his!" Cousin Ed smiled, " 'Whip Inflation Now.' That's his winning card!"

"You think it's going to work, Cousin Ed?"

"Yessir! It's done working! I rank it right up there with Evel
Kneivel's Snake River promotion!"

"But Evel Kneivel's deal was a failure."

"Failure hell! It was a whopping success! From beginning to end.
Evel done what he intended to do. And he done it big!"

"I'd like to know what was successful about it!"

"All right, I'll show you. Now Evel and his promoters told the
whole country he was going to jump the Snake River on a motorcycle, didn't they? Called it the Event of the Century."

"Yes, that's right."

"Well Evel and the whole country knowed he wasn't going to
'jump' nowhere. He was going to get hisself shot across that river.
And not on a motorcycle. In a rocket. So Evel, his promoters, and
most folks knowed the 'jump' and the 'motorcycle' was plain
hogwash. You agree?"

"Yessir, I reckon I'll have to."

"Now, what about the Event of the Century? Hell, astronauts
has been going and coming from the moon in rocketships for years.
Damn sight longer trips than that half-mile 'cross the Snake River.
Which means the Event of the Century was about as risky for Evel
as taking a nap on a couch."

"So why are you calling this such a whopping success, Cousin Ed?"

"Because it done what it was intended to do. Evel Kneivel never
intended to jump no Snake River on no motorcycle. He knowed
it; his promoters knowed it; and most of the public knowed it. He
intended just to do *one thing:* to make a potful of money. And he
did. For him and his promoters. You add up all the dollars they
made off promotion gimmicks, movies, and TV, and you'll see what
a success the Event of the Century was! All that talk about 'courage'
and 'risk' was just frosting on the cake."

"All right. I'll grant it was a great success as a hoax. But what's
Evel Kneivel's tomfoolery got to do with President Ford's WIN program?"

"Both cut out of the same cloth!" Cousin Ed snorted. "Hell, son,
Ford and his backers might not be very smart, but they ain't so
backwards that they believe a fool motto like 'Whip Inflation Now'
is going to stop inflation. Don't you know that?"

"Well, I'd like to think they're smarter than that."

"Then why do you think they launched it?"

"Tell me why, Cousin Ed."

"Same reason Evel and his top-rank promotion boys launched the Event of the Century! As a monstrous fine promotion. Great promotion! And it's going over big. Just like Evel's Snake River deal did!"

"Why, Cousin Ed, you know it's not slowing down inflation and unemployment!"

"It ain't supposed to! Wasn't never intended for that!"

"Then what is it supposed to do?"

"Make everybody feel good. And it's a success. You look around. Millions of people wearing WIN buttons. Makes them feel like they're doing something about inflation, even if they ain't. They wouldn't be wearing them fool buttons if it didn't make them feel good. Every one of them will tell you 'I'm helping President Ford Whip Inflation Now.' "

"Guess you've got a point there, Cousin Ed."

"But that ain't all! It not only makes them millions of consumers feel good to think they're fighting inflation. But it also makes the big promoters and backers of Ford feel good, too. The big monopolies and conglomerates that are making big profits off inflation, they are just like Evel Kneivel's promoters. They know what that WIN *really means*."

"What does it mean to the monopolies and conglomerates, Cousin Ed?"

"It don't mean 'Whip Inflation Now' to them birds. You can bet on that. Means just the opposite. It's the administration's way of telling them boys not to worry. Ain't going to be no antitrust legislation. Ain't going to be no enforcement of antimonopoly laws. Go right on with your control over production and distribution of oil, cars, food, and other things people have to have to live. Go right on fixing your prices, making your profits.

"It's Ford's way of saying to Big Business 'We Intend Nothing'!"

VII
A Year's Worth of Special Days

VII

These essays on the occasion of holidays include traditional "celebrations" such as New Year's Day and Thanksgiving, and also dates that pass by most years without our recognizing them, such as the anniversary of the Bill of Rights. John Henry Faulk adds a provocative twist of irony to these special days and in "The Bill of Rights" and "The Power of the People" expresses his well-known concern for constitutional guarantees.

A Sappy Happy New Year

The best advice that I can offer this New Year is that everyone should resolve to avoid conversations with a blue jay. But if you just have to chat with one, make sure that it is not Lester Blue Jay. That unhinged sinner can throw water on high spirits quicker than three collectors coming to the front door at the same time.

Yesterday, still caught up in the spirit of the season, I cracked a panful of pecans and put them out on my patio for a family of indigent squirrels. The poor creatures have had rough sledding in the food department lately. I knew they would appreciate the gesture, and I walked back in the house, warmed by the thought that I am such a charitable, kindly fellow. I had no sooner closed the sliding door than I spotted the blue shape of Lester Blue Jay, gliding through the trees and coming to a bouncy landing on the patio. He bobbed his head, put that insufferable grin of his on, and strutted over to the pan of pecans. He lit into the pecans, devouring the kernels and flinging bits of shell all over the patio.

"I'll let the rascal fill his craw. After all, it's the holiday season," I said to myself, as I slid the door open and called, "Happy New Year, Lester." He swallowed a large kernel, blinked his beady eyes, and grinned.

"Sappy New Year to you, Sappy!"

I bristled. Here I was trying to be congenial to that black-hearted thief, only to have him let fly at me with a sarcasm. I stepped out on the patio. He carefully selected the largest pecan, flitted up on a branch of the tree hanging over the patio, and began to eat the kernel with an elaborate air of indifference, taking care to drop the shells on to the patio.

"Lester," I said, "you and your sort are the cause of most of the trouble in this world! I extend season's greetings to you while you're stuffing yourself, uninvited, on my pecans, and all you can do is respond with a smart-alecky crack!"

"Oh, I do beg your pardon!" He made an exaggerated show of remorse. "I thought you were being sarcastic when you said Happy New Year!"

"Well, I wasn't," I snapped. "I was being warm and human. But you couldn't understand that!"

"You're right!" he said, measuring the distance between me and the pecans with his eye, wondering whether it was safe to dart down for another one. "I can't understand the depths of your hypocrisy. Happy New Year! Happy New Year! We're ringing the old year out and the New Year in! By bombing North Vietnam to smithereens! Got us a great new toy—a concussion bomb that kills everything within a mile of where it lands! Oh, what a Happy New Year!"

"You ungrateful scroundel," I yelled, grabbing the patio broom, "you're not happy unless you're spoiling a holiday for somebody!"

"Oh Happy New Year!" he sneered, hopping up to a higher branch, out of reach of the broom. "We're greeting the New Year with joyous slaughter again! Raining death and desolation from the sky on the heads of men, women, and children! Gouging mile-wide craters in the earth with our spanking new bomb! Oh, Happy, happy, happy!"

"Dammit, Lester, you know that the people of the United States have turned their backs on that Vietnam fiasco! We're winding the war down. Everybody but a cockeyed blue jay knows that!"

"A cockeyed blue jay—and the poor souls that are being blasted into chunks of bloody flesh!" he mocked. "Who do you think you and your sort are fooling with that stupid 'winding down the war' tripe besides yourselves? Every chee chee and blue jay in the woods sees through that piece of Madison Avenue hoakum!"

"What do you mean," I shouted, "Madison Avenue hoakum? It's a carefully planned program of withdrawal from Vietnam!"

"The American people got tired of reading about their troops being killed. The Pentagon and Nixon called in the Madison Avenue boys and said 'What do we do? This war's getting a bad name.' Madison Avenue boys said, 'Well, fix it so the American boys won't get killed, and go on with your war. Just call it by another name.' And that's just what you've done. The suffering and slaughter of those people over there are out of hearing and out of mind now. You're winding down the war! Oh Happy New Year!"

"You're a heartless cynic, Lester, and I don't have to stand here listening to your evil talk. Now git!" And I waved the broom at him.

"*I'm* a heartless cynic! *I'm* a heartless cynic!" He bounced up and down on the limb. "Why I don't light Christmas trees and creep into church muttering prayers for peace, at the very moment I'm plotting and planning to pour millions of tons of superdestruction on the heads of men, women, and children! I don't wring my hands over the plight of our POW's while perpetrating murder on their captors, guaranteeing they won't be freed, and sending more and more flyers to be POW's. I don't lull myself to sleep at night with sweet thoughts of 'winding down the war' when I know that my government is still blasting my neighbor's land into a quagmire of hellish rubble! Oh yes! What a heartless cynic I am!"

"Lester," I hissed through clenched teeth, "you know you don't care a whit about suffering humanity. You only want to jeer and make me uncomfortable."

"There it is again!" he fairly screeched. "It's *me*, Lester Blue Jay, who doesn't care about suffering humanity! It's only deeply thoughtful, Christian man who *really* cares!"

"Well, you must know that a number of the people you are ridiculing have used their best energies and prayers to stop that madness in Vietnam. And they did it at the risk of their reputations and, in some cases, freedom!"

"You're right," he jeered. "And look how magnificently you treat them! The few brave souls who long ago raised their voices in protest! You hissed them into silence with 'peacenik' and 'dove' or jailed them or drove them out of the country! And now that you agree that they were probably right—do you honor them? Respect them? No! They are still 'effete snobs' and 'subversives.' Beyond respectability."

"All right, Lester, you've succeeded in ruining my day," I said quietly. "Please take off. But I'd like to say one thing in my behalf. The majority of my neighbors now recognize the folly of the Vietnam venture. We're doing our best to put a stop to the whole sorry business. But it takes time. Rome was not built in one day."

Lester was suddenly calm, too. "You're right," he nodded. "Rome was not built in a day. But Rome and the rest of life on this earth can be destroyed in a day—or less, for that matter. And you'd better know it. This might be a Happy New Year for you. And you might even make it through to 1973. But you keep playing with war, and one of these Happy New Year's is going to be your *last* one." He took off through the trees, calling "Sappy New Year, Sappy!"

Talking Turkey

A sensible turkey has a pretty low opinion of Thanksgiving Day. But a turkey absolutely dotes on that great American holiday compared to the way my friend Joe feels about it. Joe is a Sioux Indian and proud of his heritage. He's in Texas, presently, doing some research work. Since he is alone and far from kith and kin, I invited him to have dinner with us this Thanksgiving.

"Not on your life," he replied firmly. "I wouldn't be caught dead at a Thanksgiving dinner."

"What have you got against Thanksgiving, Joe? It's a great American tradition."

"That's what I've got against it!" Joe snapped. Seeing my baffled look, Joe went on, "Look! Remember how Thanksgiving got started? Those nice Pilgrim fathers of yours came over here, loaded with puritan virtue and pious prayer. My folks met them, befriended them, introduced them to corn, and taught them how to raise it. After the first bumper crop, the Pilgrims wanted to give thanks to God, not to the Indians, for the bountiful crop. So they put on a big feast, invited my folks to come. Oh yes, to come and bring the turkey. That was the first Thanksgiving day. Also the *last* one for the Indians. By the time the second one rolled around, the pious white man had established another quaint old American tradition — killing Indians on sight.

"The white Americans went on celebrating Thanksgiving with the Indians' corn and the Indians' turkey. But without the Indians. In fact, the only attention paid to Indians on Thanksgiving was that after thanking God for all the other blessings he received the past year, the white man would also thank Him for the Indians killed."

"Goodness, Joe, you sure make the white man look mighty bad on Thanksgiving," I protested.

"The white man made the Indian look mighty dead the year 'round," Joe replied.

"You mean that first Thanksgiving was really the last one the Indians ever celebrated?" I asked.

"I guess so. After that, they probably couldn't think of anything to be thankful for."

"Well, this is going to be Thanksgiving 1972. Don't you think you ought to bury the past and its injustices? After all, we have quit killing Indians long ago."

"Yeah," Joe replied drily, "but you haven't stopped killing. You've just switched from Indians to Asians."

"Aw come on, Joe," I said. "After all, we are about to stop that war in Asia. We can all be thankful for that!"

"I've heard about our Great White Father in Washington and his 'peace with honor.' That's what it was all about, wasn't it? Peace with honor! After 56,000 Americans dead and 300,000 maimed and crippled; after more than a million Asians were dead, 100,000 of them children; 5 million homeless; after the heaviest bombing the world has ever known concentrated on a little country about the size of Mississippi; after 7 million tons of death and devastation—you are about to achieve your noble goal 'peace with honor.' You want me to come say thanks with you for winning your 'peace with honor'?"

"Well Joe, I don't blame you for feeling bitter when you put it like that. What do you think Americans ought to do over this Thanksgiving?"

"Something they never even thought of doing past Thanksgivings. Mix a little contrition into their prayers. Show just the *slightest* bit of shame for what they have done to those wretched people and their land."

"Perhaps a lot of American people will be doing that this Thanksgiving, Joe."

"Not a chance! Then they would be admitting that it was all a ghastly mistake. They would be admitting that Nixon's 'peace with honor' is a travesty on the word *honor*. And judging from that vote on November 7, most of you fine white men still think that what you have done in Southeast Asia was an exercise in Christian charity. Led by President Nixon you will all give thanks for your blessings. Your peace with honor! But you will never mention your transgressions. They are too hideous for you to contemplate."

"I hope you're wrong about that, Joe. But tell me, can't you think of one single reason to be thankful this year?"

"Oh, I suppose that there are a few. One is that my ancestors were probably luckier on Thanksgiving than the current folk you're busy killing."

"What do you mean by that?"

"Well, my folks had the comfort of knowing that on Thanksgiving Day the white man would probably be so busy praying and feasting that he wouldn't be out killing Indians that day. Now, though, with your electronic, automated methods in Asia, you can go out and get your killing done for the day, and still be home in time to give thanks and enjoy your dinner."

Legacy Letter

My dear great-great-grandson,

Bet you never thought you'd be getting a letter written a century before it reached you! Don't blame the postal service. For once, it's not their fault. I'm responsible. I'm writing about the American legacy. I want to apologize to you. We didn't intend for it to be such a sorry inheritance. It just happened. Honest.

I know you will probably grimace and mutter, "The gall of that old fraud! Trying to apologize! Apologize! After what he and his generation did to this planet! After they deliberately went on that reckless rampage of plunder, pollution, and waste! After they left us a planet of depleted resources, poisoned earth, air, and water! He wants to apologize! Wants to tell us how sorry he is! What nerve!"

But wait! Let me explain! We were not an evil people. I know by your reckoning we were. But we really weren't. The people of my generation meant well. It's just that they never stopped to think.

It happened like this, you see. We got caught up in a sort of frenzied insanity called technological growth and expansion. It started just after World War II. It consumed us, particularly in America, for we were world leaders, with accelerating intensity for decades thereafter. We called it "progress." It took the grotesque form of feverish consumption of every resource in sight, with no thought of sharing with the other peoples of the earth, let alone with posterity—you.

We invented a great Corporate Machine—senseless, sightless, heartless. We put it in charge of life on earth. We set it to gouging, digging, pumping, clawing at the earth's treasures. We knew where the treasures were located. And we knew how to get at them. We turned our Machine loose on them. Our Machine turned them into energy and goods for us to consume and waste. No matter that it fouled the water, air, and earth as it went along at its mindless marauding. Nothing was allowed to stop progress and growth. Those valiant voices that were raised in protest against the spoiling of the land, air, and water were drowned out by ridicule and scorn.

In 1973 we came up on a jolting energy crisis. Our Machine was devouring energy sources faster than they could be replaced. You well might ask, "Didn't that give you some pause? Didn't you start questioning the wisdom of your Machine? Didn't the fact that you were running out of gas so fast cause you to stop and reflect?" The answer to those questions is "No!" We just switched our source of energy and kept up our wild mad dance of consuming. Consuming and wasting. We had discovered nuclear power.

Our leaders shouted "On to Nuclear Power Plants!" And we took off after them. The nuclear plants produced energy. Along with energy, they produced invisible emissions of cancer, leukemia, and genetic mutation-causing poisons. They also produced waste materials. Waste materials of the deadliest substances known to man. Waste materials that would remain lethal to human life for a thousand years. Waste materials that, once leaked or released, could bring untold suffering and misery to millions. We thoughtfully buried the poisons in the earth. My generation never knew whether it was a successful burial. But you will! That is part of the heritage we left for you. No natural resources in the ground, as there were when we inherited the earth from our fathers. Only deposits of agonizing death for you and your children to guard.

And so for that, and the other shoddy items of our legacy to you, I apologize. If you've forgotten Thanksgiving, I can understand why.

Yours,

JHF

The Bill of Rights

December 15 ought to be a national holiday. Every citizen who values his right to go to whatever church he chooses, or to stay home on Sunday, to think and to speak as he pleases, to write and to read what he pleases, and to gather with like-minded neighbors and complain about something that does not please him, should celebrate December 15.

That is the birthday of the Bill of Rights, as the first ten amendments to our Constitution are called. The Bill of Rights gave Americans the above-mentioned rights and many more.

One of the unhappy ironies of our society today is that countless millions of Americans, any one of whom would roar in outrage if you told him that he would be compelled by law from now on to go to a particular church and embrace a particular religion, have not the foggiest notion of how the Bill of Rights came to be part of the supreme law of the land. And just about that many have only the faultiest sort of notion about the full meaning of its provisions. This goes for some of our leading public officials—newspaper editors, judges, and others—who should know better. Yet the freedoms guaranteed by our Bill of Rights affect the lives of all the citizens of this land every day.

The remarkable assemblage of gentlemen who swatted flies, slapped mosquitoes, sweated, and labored all that long hot summer of 1787 in Philadelphia to construct our charter of government, the Constitution, finished it up, polished it, and sent it to the thirteen states to be ratified in September 1787.

Setting up a federal government that would supersede the state governments from King George and the British Parliament, they were not about to trust their newfound liberties to a strong central government, even one of their own making. "Liberty" and "Freedom" were on every man's lips, and right off the cry went up that the proposed Constitution contained no Bill of Rights. The proponents of the Constitution, particularly James Madison, agreed with the complaints and promised that the very first order of business of the new Congress, if the Constitution was accepted, would be to make a Bill of Rights a part of it.

That's exactly what was done. Congress fell to and framed the first ten amendments to the Constitution, debating every detail and word of each of their provisions, and sending them out to the states for ratification in 1789. The people had demanded, and the framers had constructed, a wall that protected the individual and his freedom to enjoy certain natural rights against the arbitrary use of power by the government so long as the Constitution stood.

Actually, as James Madison and Thomas Jefferson pointed out, the guarantee of these individual freedoms was the only way to make the whole idea of free men governing themselves work. The Bill of Rights was the heartbeat of our free republic. The central idea of the Bill of Rights might be said to be that a man is truly free only if he does not have to ask himself if he is free.

I grew up, like most Americans do, taking my Bill of Rights freedoms for granted. They were mine to enjoy without let or hindrance. I knew this. But like a great many other Americans, I didn't know that the freedoms also extended to people who differed with me.

For instance, the right to think and speak as I pleased was the freedom that I exercised most often. But it was the freedom I resented most when it was exercised by the wrong people—like my parents and sisters. It appalled me that people as misinformed and ignorant as they were assumed the right to express opinions like, "Johnny, you don't know what you're talking about." Many times, had I the power and authority, I would have jailed the lot of them. The gentlemen who bequeathed to us our Bill of Rights knew that there would be lots and lots of people coming along, in and out of government, who felt just as I did about those who held contrary, unpopular opinions. They wisely forbade us the legal power to shut up anyone, friend or foe.

I was grown and long out of school before I came to understand the spaciousness of the Bill of Rights. I could readily understand that it protected the ideas that we cherish and love. It took a lot more understanding for me to realize that it protects with equal force the ideas that we abhor and despise. When I came to this realization, the true genius of the first ten amendments became plain to me and deepened my awe and respect for those who passed them down to us.

Time and again, during the nearly two centuries that the Bill of Rights has been the law of this land, fear and panic have at times caused us to turn our backs on its guarantees. Congress had repeatedly given way and sought to render its protections null and void. But each time, as the fears subsided, and calmer times prevailed, the American people have rededicated themselves to its principles. We have recognized each time that the defects lie in ourselves, not in the Bill of Rights. Let us hope that it will continue to stand as a monument to the inspired conviction of our founding fathers that Americans, free from the threat of government repression, will always have the courage to defend those freedoms for all citizens, here, now, and yet to be born.

The Power of the People

Come December 1973, we will celebrate the bicentennial of the Boston Tea Party. That event, of course, is widely regarded as the spark that flew up and down the Atlantic seaboard, firing up the spirit of independence in the American colonies. It led directly to the Declaration of Independence three years later and to its aftermath, the American Revolution, called, with good reason, the Glorious Revolution.

In 1787 our founding fathers gathered in Philadelphia to embody the principles and ideals for which the revolution had been fought into a charter of government. After a summer of tedious debate, endless discussion, and compromise, they ended up with that cornerstone of self-government, the Constitution of the United States. It was, of course, a completely revolutionary document, the likes of which the world had never before seen. It was a contract between free and equal men, providing for a society in which the citizens would be sovereign and the government the servant. Officeholders in the new government would be called "public servants," and whatever powers and privileges went with the office they held would *always* belong to the people, all the people, of the United States. The people could alter, amend, or, if they desired, abolish the terms of the charter. But no officeholder, however much power his office bestowed upon him, could change that charter by even a jot.

At the time the charter became operative, the rest of the Western world was dominated by governments that were sovereign and people who were subjects. And many powerful European leaders sneered at the notion that the United States could last (even ten years) with the people trying to govern themselves by the terms of such an absurd document.

Now, some 180-odd years later, we can say that the proof of the pudding is in the eating. We've made it. And not because we have not come through some rough, indeed perilous, times. The history of each of the amendments to the Constitution, including the first ten, our Bill of Rights, is invariably the story of a self-governing people determined to correct what they perceive to be injustice and error. In fact, one might say that each amendment added to the Constitution was an attempt of the American people to expand and extend the blessings of self-government and its manifold benefits to an ever-wider circle of our citizenry.

From time to time, those holding offices of trust in our government have forgotten or ignored the limitations that our charter of government places on the individual holding the office. Such persons have used the powers of the office as though they were theirs personally, rather than powers belonging to the people. Every single time that has happened, the offending officeholder has been rewarded with a stern reprimand by the people. Not a one has ever gotten away with the usurpation of power. That is, I am convinced, because the office is invariably bigger, more important, and a lot more permanent than the officeholder.

The powers that go with the highest office in the land, the presidency, are awesome indeed. But they belong to the people, all the people, still. The man who holds that office and forgets whom those powers really belong to does so at his own peril. As we have seen.

VIII
Giving the Nuclear Issue a Bad Name

VIII

One of the challenges for the humorist is to take on a cause and not lose a humorous grip on it. For John Henry Faulk, that challenge is the greatest when facing the issue of nuclear war. Is there anything funny about a potential holocaust? No, but Faulk shows us that there is much need for the humorist's needle in showing us the folly that faces us all. To help him, he invokes his backyard blue jay along with Mr. Stump Tucker and of course Cousin Ed Snodgrass, the crackerbarrel philosopher who will always rise to a challenge if someone is needed to play out the foibles of the human race.

A Bird's-Eye View of Mankind

The closer the AEC got to the date for setting off the nuclear test on Amchitka Island, the more apprehensive I got about the deal. The possibility of the biggest man-made blast to date in the earth's bowels made me uneasy. So when the Sunday morning papers carried the glad tidings in their headlines—"BLAST OF CANNIKER SUCCESSFUL, SAFE"—I was naturally relieved. While the details of the test were not altogether reassuring, the jubilation of the scientists and military folk who had run the show was sort of contagious, so I relaxed.

I was still in something approaching a state of euphoria when I went out in the yard to fill my bird feeders. The usual squadron of squirrels was frisking about in the trees, eager to pitch in and start emptying the first feeder before I could get the last one filled. Several cardinals and song sparrows in residence and a small flock of visiting lesser goldfinches sported about in the branches, staying back until I finished filling the feeders and got out of the way. They enjoy the feeders but not my company. As I shook the last of the grain out of my bucket on the ground for the four shy Inca doves that sat quietly in a nearby bush, I noticed that one of the feeders was leaking the grain out. I took it down to see what the trouble was.

That's where I made my mistake. Anytime I stop to fool around out there near the feeders, Lester Blue Jay spots me and comes sailing over for the sole purpose, I am convinced, of ruining my day. And sure enough, before I could even examine the feeder, here he came, winging through the trees gleefully and coming to a landing on a low limb about two feet over my head. There he perched, bobbing his head and grinning with blue jay mischief. Lester is not only a noisy gossip but also by all odds the most obnoxious show-off in the whole neighborhood. He never misses a chance to come over and make a fool out of me in front of the other birds. He has inherited a triple supply of all the smug arrogance and raucus bad manners that are the hallmark of his tribe.

"Great show yesterday, Johnny!" he began, his voice grating with blue jay sarcasm. "Really pulled off a beaut. You must be brimming with pride. I hear you managed to let go with something in the neighborhood of five million tons of TNT. Must be mighty proud of yourselves."

I tried to ignore him, hoping that he would go away. I bent over the feeder and said nothing. I should have known better. He whacked his beak on the limb a couple of licks, pretending to clean it, cocked a malicious eye at me and badgered, "What's the matter? Cat got your tongue?" and let out with a squawking jay laugh. The cardinals and sparrows tittered. In spite of my resolution to ignore him, I snapped.

"I was feeling just fine. Just splendid! Until a certain smart-aleck blue jay showed up, uninivited. Now you get going before I heave this feed bucket at your empty head."

"My, my! Aren't we testy today! And after all the grand testing yesterday!" he taunted. "I thought you would be glowing and crowing with pride, like Jim Schlesinger, the chairman of the AEC, is. Why, just look what a great boom you made yesterday! And without blowing the top of the earth off like a kettle lid! What a brilliant achievement!"

"Listen, Lester," I said, "that was a complete success. It didn't do a speck of harm."

"Nor even spill a teacupful of fallout," he mocked. "Even if it did leave clouds of it to seep through the earth's fissures. How wonderful! As Schlesinger said, now you can introduce the Spartan missile to your weapon inventory! Simply superb!"

"I suppose you know more about such matters than President Nixon and the Supreme Court do. They endorsed the blast," I countered.

"Say now, ain't that just peachy!" he hopped about cackling. "Jim-dandy, that's what it is! Now you can slaughter millions of your kind in one glorious explosion. How nice."

"You're probably disappointed that somebody didn't get killed by the test yesterday," I said snappily.

"Not me," he screeched, "I couldn't care less. But I hear the buzzards were disappointed. They figured on a great feast."

"You are revolting, Lester," I said.

"Look who's calling *who* revolting!" he said, bouncing up and down on the limb and preening himself before the other birds. "They dedicate their best minds, their greatest energies, their richest resources to creating a bomb that can and will blow them all to smithereens — and take most other life on earth with them. Then they have the gall to call us revolting!"

"Listen, you pecan-stealing, little-bird-bullying, empty-headed blue jay," I shouted. "You don't know anything about national defense or technological progress. And I'm not going to stand here arguing with you. They made their test. It was successful and they won't have to test it any more."

"Until they want a bigger one next week," he sneered.

"You bet they will, if technological progress and national defense call for it," I said defiantly. I hated to think that a blue jay, particularly that troublemaking numbskull, could get under my skin by running down my species, make me say things I didn't mean. I knew that it was impossible to embarrass a blue jay, shame him into leaving. So I decided to leave myself. As I started away he guffawed, "What do you call it? National defense and technological progress? Us birds call it by another name — lunacy."

I was red-faced at being run in the house by an egotistical, opinionated blue jay. I knew the squirrels and the other birds were snickering and laughing. I mumbled, "I'm going to wait in the house until that loudmouth leaves."

Lester ruffled his feathers, cocked his beak at a jaunty angle, and screeched, "You're not the only one who'll be waiting. The buzzards are waiting, too. Patient lot, buzzards are. They know their day is coming."

Enough is Enough

"How would you like for me to be able to kill *you* forty times," Mr. Stump Tucker demanded the other morning when I went over to visit him, "and know that *you* couldn't kill *me* but just twenty-five times?" We were out near one of his hog pens. He had just finished feeding a couple of dozen pigs several buckets of slop, a good part of which was still plastered over his clothes and his countenance.

Ordinarily, Mr. Stump Tucker sticks strictly to the one and only subject that he has made his life's work: hogs. Some years ago, he had confided to me that he was the world's leading authority on hog raising, and had no use for the animal husbandry experts. They studied books instead of hogs. As he put it, "If you're going to git anywheres with a hog, you've got to know hogs, not books. I've knowed a jillion hogs. But I never knowed a hog to write a book. Why? Because a hog is too busy being a hog to write books. Look at it this way. Who knows most about being a hog? A hog! Who knows most 'bout what's on a hog's mind? 'Bout how a hog feels? A hog! That's why I stay clear of them so-called agriculture experts down at A&M. Stick with hogs, if you want to learn hogs! That's *my* motto."

So the other morning when he launched into the subject of international affairs, I was as surprised at his interest as I was puzzled at how to answer his question of how I would feel if he could kill me several times more than I could kill him. His query to me had been triggered by my innocent attempt to make a joke. I had said, "Those hogs are as fat as some of the overfed defense contractors in the country, Mr. Stump."

"Let me tell you something," he declared, fixing me with a fiery glare, "I'm plumb agitated over this country's ignernce and indifference on that there defense business! Mr. Melvin Laird and them Pentygone experts is a-warning us. But we ain't listening."

"What do you mean by that?" I asked.

"That folks like you are lettin' down our defenses!" he answered. "Gittin' overconfident and self-satisfied just because we've got a few nuclear weapons."

"A few!" I exclaimed, "We've got an arsenal that can destroy all life on earth several times! So have the Russians!"

"You ain't been studyin' this here like I have," he assured me, "or you would know what's really going on. Mr. Laird and the defense boys is the ones that *really* know. Them's the ones I listent to. They've studied them Russians. Know the rascals. Lived 'em and breathed 'em, like I've lived and breathed hogs. They understand 'em inside out, up and down, and sideways."

"What do you think they know that the rest of us don't know, Mr. Tucker?"

"They know psychology. They know the one thing most any foreigner you meet wants to do is git around behind your back and stick a knife in it. And they know the Russians is the worst of all 'bout that. Only them Russians won't be packing no knife when they git behind you. They'll be packing a nuclear bomb. Once they git a lick at you with it, you might as well throw in your chips. You're out of the game!"

"I must say, Mr. Tucker," I commented, "the whole weird thing is a nightmare to me. This idiotic stockpiling of death and destruction has lost any logical meaning it ever had."

That is when he propounded his question about how I'd like it if he could kill me forty times and I could only kill him twenty-five times.

"Well," I answered, after I thought of it a bit, "once you kill me the first time, it don't make much difference how many more times you could do it!"

"There you are!" he exclaimed. "That's just what Melvin Laird's been a-pointin' out! You and these here other ignernt folks don't know the score! That's just what them Red Rascals over in Russia is a-plannin' on you thinkin'! Lull yourself to sleep with the happy thought we can kill all them twenty-five times and they can't kill us but sixteen times. That's what Melvin Laird is trying to point out. That's where we are now. Next week we liable to wake up and discover it's just the opposite. We'll still be dozing along at that twenty-five times figger. And the Russians will of shot passed and gone up to thirty-five or forty times! I'll tell you it chills my blood! Chills my blood to think that people can't understand what Mr. Laird and the Pentygone boys is talking about!"

"It does mine, too, Mr. Tucker," I replied.

Giving Nuclear War a Bad Name

My cousin Ed Snodgrass has done a great deal of thinking about the problem of nuclear war. As you know, the administration has set forth a program that says it is quite possible for us to have a limited nuclear war. Then there's the other side, drumming up support for a freeze on all nuclear weapons.

The country is very confused now about where we stand. The administration says we need more weapons than ever before, more horrifying and terrible weapons. Yet another group is saying, "Look, you've moved mankind to the very edge of destruction. You have almost moved to the point where you can't turn back and all life on Earth is threatened by this horror."

And over it all is the magnificent spirit of Einstein shaking his head sadly and saying, "Don't you know that when you released the power of the atom, everything changed in man's history except his modes of thinking? Thus you drift towards indescribable disaster."

So what we have done is arrive at a point where there is no choice but to change mankind's modes of thinking. Or so I thought until Cousin Ed Snodgrass explained it all to me the other day.

"Johnny, thank God for Jerry Falwell and his Moral Majority. He's cleared up my thinking so much, you know. Bless his Christian heart. They'll tell every lie they can on Jerry Falwell, just to hurt his feelings. But I've done a study on the Moral Majority, Johnny, and they've done so much good.

"You know they say the Moral Majority is full of bigots—that's just a pop-eyed lie. Jerry Falwell and the Moral Majority is for brotherhood. White brotherhood, of course. Let brotherhood be amongst those people that likes theirselves. That's all Jerry Falwell says.

"Why, Jerry Falwell started a Brotherhood Week and we was going good until it turned out these old women's lib people and gays and everything else wanted to be included. That just ruined Brotherhood Week for us.

"And Johnny, the thing that Jerry Falwell has taught me is: don't be afraid of nuclear war. They say that Ronald Reagan's for nuclear war. Jerry Falwell points out that we don't want nuclear war *here*— we want nuclear war over *there*. He don't believe in Americans getting killed, just Russians. You say, well, he just seems to hate Russians so. 'Course he does.

"That's the wonderful thing about Jerry Falwell. He knows how to hate. But you'll notice one thing about him: he always tries to hate in a Christian way.

"Now, Ronald Reagan knows that nuclear war is dangerous. Highly dangerous. You say, now wait a minute. Then why is he coming out for nuclear war? That's the whole point. It has to be a special kind of nuclear war, a limited nuclear war is the only kind he believes in. Limit it to somewhere else. That's the only safe kind of nuclear war you can have today.

"I'd just like to ask these people who are criticizing the administration all the time, how would they like it if every time they tried to go to bed they had somebody peeking through their window of vulnerability? That's what poor Ronald Reagan has to put up with. Somebody peeking through his window of vulnerability, trying to find out all his secrets.

"I'll say this, people don't understand Russia. They're ignorant and don't understand what Ronald Reagan is doing. You hear these old liberals and Democrats up in Congress say, 'We got enough nuclear power to blow up every man, woman, and child in Russia twenty-five times. Let's lean back. Let's quit spending money on nuclear weapons. They can't kill us but twelve times. We're way ahead of them.'

"Do you think Ronald Reagan would listen to that? You think Caspar Weinberger and George Bush would listen? Oh, no, they know better than that. What if we have an all-out nuclear war and find out the Russians can kill us thirty times and we're still back there at twenty-five? How would you feel then? It would be too late to go to Ronald Reagan and say, we want to apologize, Mr. Reagan. He'd say, 'Kiss my foot.'

"I'll tell you what this whole nuclear freeze thing is about, Johnny. I made a study of it. This bilateral nuclear freeze business ain't a thing in the world but them same old protestors and peaceniks that kept a-deviling poor old Lyndon Johnson back during the Vietnam War. They kept that up till they just ruined a perfectly good war in Vietnam and now they started the same thing on nuclear war. And what they're going to do is to keep on until they give nuclear war a bad name."

IX
An Island Down South

IX

In 1983 Faulk requested press credentials from the Charleston Gazette *to travel to Cuba. His report on life in the Communist country was published in three installments in the Charleston newspaper.*

I went down to Cuba not long ago. I was there for only two weeks, but that was quite enough time for me to discover that there are actually two Cubas.

One is the Cuba that I have been learning about in the American media these last two decades: grim and gray and forbidding. This is the Cuba that I expected to encounter. The other Cuba is a tropical island about the size of Tennessee, shaped like an alligator, with close to ten million people, all of whom are pretty much on an equal footing economically and socially, and most of them, judging from the ones I met, a friendly, warmhearted lot. This is the Cuba that I found on my visit.

At the José Marte airport in Havana, our Cubana Airlines jet from Mexico City landed only moments before an Air Florida jet from Miami. One of the passengers from Miami, a middle-aged lady with bluish gray hair and in generous proportions, wore two Western hats, one on top of the other. As we lined up to go through immigration, she was directly in front of me. I asked her why she wore two hats. She answered pleasantly, with a strong Spanish accent, "These are gifts for my father and brother. They love Western hats. They can't get them here in Cuba." She told me that she had left Cuba fifteen years ago and is now an American citizen living in Florida. Her parents and her brother remained in Cuba. She comes as often as possible to visit them. She always brings them some gifts from the United States. "Things like blouses and hats. The Communists won't allow us to bring in big gifts like hi-fi sets and color TV. They do not want their people to have those."

She then related to me, with some distress, that her parents and her brother actually chose to remain in Cuba, although she and her husband had urged them to come to Florida. "They're so stubborn," she lamented, "they like to live in prison."

I asked her if Cuba was really as bad as all that. "Worse!" she responded with conviction. "It's Communist hell. No freedom. No liberty. You must be on guard against Castro spies everywhere. You cannot speak any criticism of the monster Castro. You can get arrested for just thinking wrong thoughts in Cuba. Be very careful."

The fact that she was at that moment in Cuba, confiding these awful truths to a complete stranger, did not seem to strike her as an irony.

Two friends of mine from Texas, Fred Baldwin and Wendy Watriss, both excellent photojournalists, were with me for the trip. We were met at the airport by a handsome mulatto named Solomon. He was an outgoing jolly man of about thirty-five who carried an astonishing compendium of information about Cuba in his head. Most of it had to do with the accomplishments of the Cuban revolution. Solomon tended to become rhapsodic on the subject.

He told us that both his parents were illiterate, very poor rural farm workers. That is, they were illiterate before the revolution. So was Solomon, who was fourteen years old when Castro took over. Now both his parents can read and write; so can all of their eight children. An elder brother is a pediatrician in Matanzas. Two of his sisters are schoolteachers in Havana. His parents are still poor, but they are much happier. They have security against hunger and disease now. That is why they support the revolution, Solomon pronounced firmly.

Cuba is not a consumer society. One thing it means is that they don't hawk consumer goods of any kind on billboards or signs. It is one of the first things you notice about Cuba as you drive toward town from the airport. What billboards one does see are selling patriotic slogans and urging "Education and Production," and "The Revolution teaches proletarian courtesy to all."

It was rush hour, and the traffic was much heavier than I had any idea it would be. Solomon was driving a new Russian Lada sedan, just a fraction smaller than my Buick Skylark back in Texas. It carried four very comfortably. The streets were abuzz with Japanese Toyotas, Russian Ladas, Italian Fiats, and other European makes that I could not identify. "Cubans like their cars," he commented. Indeed they did. They held on to them, too. We kept seeing products of Detroit from around the 1950s—Dodges, Pontiacs, Chevys, and others, all reflecting loving care by their owners. Repair parts have not been available since the United States clamped its embargo on Cuba twenty years ago.

"We resent your *bloqueo* [blockade]," Solomon declared, as we discussed the problem of spare parts for American cars. "It has worked a great hardship on us. The United States is hurt too." Then he recited some figures to prove his point. Before the ban in 1962, Cuba did more than $1 billion worth of trade a year with the United

States. Cuba was the principal Latin American trading partner of the United States. Since the embargo, all trade has stopped flat. Cuba has now developed trade relations with the Soviet Union, which takes most of its sugar crop. It also has trade relations with Japan, Canada, and Western Europe. Cuba spends millions of dollars on transportation equipment in Japan and Spain, millions on pesticides from Switzerland, and millions each year on grain from Canada.

"It doesn't even make business sense," Solomon shook his head. "Your business people could be making millions on the Cuban market. You sell computers and technology to the Soviet Union and China, but you won't even sell toilet paper to Cuba. It's crazy!"

This is a sentiment we were to hear repeatedly during our stay. We asked about rationing in Cuba. "It's a way of life in Cuba," Solomon admitted. "Clothes, shoes, and the like come in one single style. No competing brands like you have in your capitalist consumer society." He told us that milk and meat are strictly rationed. However, he was eager to point out that most foodstuff and all luxury items prior to the revolution were beyond the reach of most of the poor in Cuba, so they might as well have been rationed then, no?

It was on the subject of public health and education that Solomon really became eloquent. Before the revolution, nearly 50 percent of the people of Cuba were illiterate. Malnutrition and disease were the constant lot of the poor. A lifetime of poverty and no hope for improvement were universal facts of life for millions of Cubans. Then came Fidel and his bearded friends. The great landholdings were confiscated, the huge estates broken up. Land was given to the poor. Housing, schools, and hospitals were built all over the island. Education and public health services were available to all.

Today, Solomon said proudly, the life expectancy is seventy-two years. Everyone in Cuba has the equivalent of at least an eighth-grade education ("One of the miracles of education in the world," he declared). There is no unemployment. No worker pays more than 10 percent of his salary for rent. Movies and concerts all cost less than a dollar. All workers get one month's vacation a year, with the government picking up part of the tab at hotels and beach resorts. "It's communism," Solomon said with a laugh, "but most Cubans like it."

"Are you a member of the Communist Party, Solomon?" I asked.

"Of course!" he answered as though I had asked if he breathed air. "But," he added, almost apologetically, "I have much to read and study before I can be a good party member. A good party member puts the revolution first in his thoughts."

I could not imagine how Solomon could possibly put the revolution any firster in his thoughts than he was already doing, but I made no comment.

We drove through a section of Havana called Miramar, along wide, tree-lined boulevards by magnificent homes set in wide lawns and lovely flower gardens. It was the section where the wealthy of Havana lived before Castro came. Many of the homes are now used for foreign embassies and state offices. Some have been divided into workers' apartments. A few are still inhabited by their original owners.

"If a wealthy family supported the revolution," Solomon explained, "that family could keep its home. I know a doctor and his wife who were very wealthy. They both supported the revolution. They still do. They have the same home that they had before the revolution. Even the same beautiful paintings are still there. He wears sandals now. He supports the people. Of course, no person can own two homes. Just one."

The Riviera Hotel, where we stayed in Havana, is a neo–Las Vegas type resort hotel. It was built by United States racketeer Meyer Lansky as a gambling place and resort on the north shore of Havana in the 1950s. This was the period when Meyer and the Mafia were well on the way to converting Havana into the brothel of the Caribbean and making it the international headquarters for organized crime, during the last years of dictator Fulgencio Batista.

The Riviera, the Capri, the Havana Hilton (now called Havana Libre), and other luxury hotels of that period were actually unintended gifts. They were all completed during the freewheeling economic expansion days of Batista when foreign investments ruled Cuba's economy. Castro and his boys took them over and have run them ever since. And kept them well-staffed and up to snuff. They do a sizable tourist business.

A Canadian businessman remarked to me at breakfast in the Riviera dining room one morning when I expressed surprise at seeing so many tourists in Havana, "Yes, hordes of Canadians spend their vacations on the beaches here. It is cheaper than Florida by far. So do many Europeans. You Americans are the only ones who seem afraid to come."

In the hotel lobbies and at various Havana restaurants to which our party went, we encountered a regular United Nations parade of people. Some, of course, were there on business, but many were there for a season in the sun. Fred, Wendy, and I discussed the phenomenon: of all the things pro and con that we had ever heard of Castro's Cuba, its being a tourist haven was not one.

By the second day in Cuba, the three of us were agreeing that the Cuba that we were seeing firsthand was startlingly different from what we had expected. Take the cultural life of Havana. It was fairly pulsing. We had our choice between the Havana Symphony, the Cuban Ballet, a great Latin American Film Festival, and a dozen or so little theaters, cabarets, and revues. Señor Santiago Alvarez, the director of Cuban Film Industry, invited us to be his guests for an evening at the film festival. We went to the showing of films from every Latin American country except Chile. There were several film people from Chile there, but they were refugees from Pinochet's Chile living in Cuba now.

Most of the films were quite sophisticated documentaries on a wide variety of subjects. One that attracted keen attention was a documentary done by a team of Peruvian filmmakers on the guerilla forces in El Salvador. I doubt that anything like it will be seen anytime soon in the United States. It showed guerrilla forces armed exclusively with United States weapons and equipment. The camera took the audience along to an actual encounter between guerrilla and government forces. We saw the stores of ammunition and arms that were captured, as well as government troops who surrendered. Some of these elected to remain with the rebel forces. A viewer of the film could not but wonder why the Salvadoran rebel forces, most of whom were barefoot and in ragged clothes, would risk having guns and ammunition shipped in from Nicaragua and Cuba when they repeatedly captured more American equipment from the government forces than they could haul off.

You would think that Cuba would win at least one passing mark from President Reagan. Its work ethic is everything that Reagan and friends preach: every able-bodied man is required to work. Get a job or go to jail is the rule. And it is enforced. There are, we learned, shady characters who live by their wits rather than by the sweat of their brows, black marketeers who traffic in stereos, tapes, and other forbidden items. Most of the thieves, we were told, had gone to the United States in 1980.

Interestingly enough, the great exodus from Mariel in 1980 attracted far more attention in Cuba than it did in the United States. What was treated by the Carter administration and the United States press as a great coup for United States standing internationally — 100,000 people fleeing Cuban tyranny to American freedom — was viewed as just the opposite by a British newsman whom we met for drinks. He was a longtime Castro watcher.

"Fidel really got one over on Carter that time. He unloaded thousands of welfare cases and hustlers on the U.S.," our friend observed.

"You know, of course, that Fidel has had a longstanding rule that anyone who does not want to stay in Cuba and help the revolution is free to leave." He then explained that the trouble has been with the United States' immigration policy; at times it would relax, and then be restricted. In 1980 Carter opened the floodgates. Everybody who wanted to go took off. There is a strong prejudice against homosexuality in Cuba. The macho image is cherished there. So gays departed in droves. So did flocks of petty thieves and other anti-social sorts. Street crime in Havana dropped 50 percent after the Mariel exodus, according to police records. Castro had simply shipped a lot of his problems to President Carter.

We asked our British friend, after he expressed his strong dislike of the restrictions on a free press and free speech that prevailed in the one-party state of Cuba, how he sized up the public support the government enjoyed.

"No way of estimating it," he responded. "They don't have public opinion polls in Cuba, you know. I would guess that the majority of the people support it, however. After all, it could hardly carry on if they did not, could it?"

He said that he had heard quite a bit of grumbling and complaining about the government bureaucracy. It seemed to be something of a national pastime in Cuba.

"What you do not hear," he assured us, "is criticism of the Communist Party and its goals. That kind of criticism is not tolerated in Cuba."

"What if I stood up and denounced Castro as a bloody tyrant?" I asked.

"You would be in jail very quickly. Or tossed out of Cuba on your ear." He smiled, adding, "about as quickly as a Cuban would be deported if he stood up in the United States and denounced President Reagan."

Lionel Martin is an American journalist, a correspondent for

Reuters and stringer for ABC News, who has lived in Havana for the past twenty years. He is something of a student on the life of Fidel Castro. I had dinner at his home one evening. When I remarked that I actually knew very little about Fidel Castro—what kind of background he came from, his education—and that what little I did know I had learned from hostile sources, Martin nodded.

"I know what you mean. And that is a shame. The people of the United States deserve to know more about Castro than what his enemies say about him."

"But he is a Marxist, isn't he?" I asked. "And doesn't that mean he sees the world and history through the narrow tunnel of Marxist doctrine?"

"There are at this point in history at least a dozen countries in the world claiming to be adherents to Marxist doctrines," Martin explained. "Fidel Castro is a Marxist. But he is his own kind of communist—a Cuban Communist. That's what the American press has failed to examine, to understand. No one in the American media has bothered to study the man, Fidel Castro, to understand why he has made a success of the Cuban revolution in spite of seemingly overwhelming odds."

"I thought he maintained his position in Cuba because he had pretty much closed the door to any political competition in Cuba," I said.

"Indeed he has done that," Martin agreed. "But I was talking about his success against the efforts of the United States to dismantle his revolution. You will admit that it took enormous political skill and wisdom to survive against the massive economic and military agression that the CIA and the United States government have directed against the Castro government. It would be in the American people's best interest to understand the man's genius, if only to better cope with him."

He then gave me a book that he had written on Castro. I admitted to him, somewhat lamely, that it was the first book that I had ever seen, let alone planned to read, on the life of Fidel Castro. I asked Martin if he had any inside information on why Castro sent troops to Angola and maintained such close ties with the Nicaraguan government, sending teachers, military advisers, and scientists there.

"There are many reasons. As for Angola, I think one of the main reasons is that at least one-third of the Cuban population is of African descent. Castro wants to express solidarity with the Angolan blacks against the white South African government.

"In the case of Nicaragua, most Cubans will tell you that Cubans strongly identify with Nicaragua. The histories of their revolutions are identical. Both struggled against a brutal and corrupt U.S.-supported dictator: Batista in Cuba, Somoza in Nicaragua. The way the Cuban government sees it, both have had to contend with the high-handed arrogance of those imperialist forces in the United States that desire their downfall. Cuba feels duty-bound to give every assistance to Nicaragua. Cuba will not desert Nicaragua in its hour of need. You will see."

As I was leaving, Martin commented,"Don't mistake the point that I was trying to make. Castro and his government have made mistakes—many of them. And they've made some beauts. Even some pretty silly ones. They prohibited alcoholic beverages because they thought drinking interfered with workers' production. Prohibition was a dismal failure. They dropped it, and production actually picked up." (I found out that they have another means of curbing drinking in Cuba; they take a couple of hours to bring your drink after you order! It's impossible to get more than two drinks a night!)

Cubans are almost as proud of their progress against racism as they are of their achievements in education and public health. Before the revolution, persons with so much as a trace of African blood were barred from most of the exclusive clubs, and blacks all over Cuba suffered economic prejudice. An all-out campaign was waged against prejudicial treatment—socially, politically, and economically—by the Castro government. It is now said that racism has all but disappeared from Cuban society.

I was amazed that Cuba has a space program. The first flight into outer space by a Cuban was in conjunction with the Soviet Union. The first Cuban cosmonaut was Arnoaldo Tamayo Mendes, a Cuban black whose parents were illiterate laborers in Camarones, out in the Guantanamo Province. Cubans like to point out that the first black man ever to travel in outer space was a Cuban.

Several people told me that I must be sure to meet Feijoo. Feijoo could explain Cuba to me, as it was before and after the revolution. He came to see me at the Riviera Hotel one evening. We met in a bar since the Riviera, like all the other Havana hotels, has an absolute, iron-clad, no-exceptions rule against any guest in the hotel inviting anyone—male or female—to visit in his or her hotel room.

Samuel Feijoo (pronounced Fayho), known far and wide in Cuba to old and young alike by his last name only, is a wiry little man of slightly simian countenance, piercing blue eyes, and a bald pate. He is as lean and muscular as a whippet and can run as fast as one in a fifty-yard dash. He was a bantamweight boxer in his youth, and even now he is given to sudden ducking and weaving and dancing while feinting blows at an imaginary opponent. It's his way of letting you know that for all his sixty-nine years, he is still to be reckoned with in the ring, I suppose.

Feijoo is a poet, a novelist, a painter, a caricaturist, an essayist, and most of all, a folklorist. He has collected hundreds of folk songs and folk stories of the *campesinos*, the rural poor in Cuba. He is a definitive authority on the *decima*, a folk-art form of spontaneous song and poetry created on the spot by *campesino* folk artists to celebrate a person or an event.

Feijoo, I was to discover, is something of a national treasure in Cuba. The evening that I met him, he raised a glass in my direction and called, "I drink your health with butterfly milk."

"Why do you drink butterfly milk?" I asked.

"Because I cannot stand cockroach milk," he replied quickly. Feijoo came from a well-to-do background, but his sympathies have always been with the rural poor. Their hunger and poverty touched him deeply. Now that they have more security and plenty to eat, he is a dedicated champion of the revolution and glorifies Castro.

Feijoo was a friend of Pablo Picasso. He owns several Picassos. And Picasso, before he died, was the proud possessor of several Feijoos. Feijoo was also a close friend of Ernest Hemingway, whom he calls "Papa," as most other Cubans do. He directed us to the Floradita Bar and Restaurant, a favorite Hemingway drinking headquarters.

"Ah, Papa loved Cuba. He loved the people. Papa supported our revolution. He loved Fidel. They were close friends. Papa said Fidel was a great statesman."

Feijoo invited us to come see him autograph his latest book, an anthology. We found out when we arrived that it was a bit more than a Feijoo autograph party. It was actually the annual Cuban Book Fair, which runs for two weeks each year and is held on a wide avenue blocked off at both ends. Dozens of bookstalls lined each side, with signs telling the subject of the books in the individual stalls. "Science and Technical," "Art and Literature," etc.

Thousands of people, old and young, browsed through the stalls. Some gathered at stalls where authors were reading from their works. Others queued up to have books autographed.

Feijoo was seated at an elevated table, busily autographing books for people in a queue that extended for nearly a block. Feijoo's works were obviously very popular.

When we approached, he continued to write so Fred and Wendy could get some photographs of him in action. Then he stood up, stretched, and announced to those still waiting in line, "My finger is dying. I can't sign any more books today."

To those who protested, he said firmly, "My book is just as good without my name written in it as it is with my name scribbled in the flyleaf. I wrote it for you to read, not for me to autograph."

I commented to Feijoo on the size of the crowd at the fair.

"I would say," I smiled, "that book fairs in Cuba rank right up there with Castro's speeches when it comes to drawing a crowd."

"We have," Feijoo said solemnly, "published over five million books since the revolution. Look over there. There is a quote from Fidel." He pointed at a banner across the entrance of the fair. It said "We do not say 'believe us.' We say read."

The authorities try to make that possible for all, it seems. Feijoo's book, as did most of the others at the fair, cost less than a dollar.

Feijoo gave us a guided tour out through the green farmlands of central Cuba and down to Cienfuegos, 100 miles to the south. We drove along a great modern superhighway that runs the whole length of the island. We drove past wide, fertile fields of sugar cane, groves of mango trees, clumps of Cuban pine trees, banana groves, past eighteen-wheeler trucks and rigs hauling produce, and past fields where men plowed with oxen. The old Cuba blended with the new, and although we saw many thatched-roofed shacks and drab villages, there was an air of optimism in the people.

We went one night to hear some of Feijoo's favorite folk singers. He declared to us that the singers we would hear were masters of the *decima*. The best in Cuba. Indeed, the world.

We gathered in the sparsely furnished front room of a hospitable, gentle family of *campesinos*. A heavy-set, middle-aged *campesino* with shaggy eyebrows and a severe frown marched to the middle of the room and cut loose in a hoarse roar that sent Feijoo and the Cubans present into fits of laughter. The words, in idiomatic Spanish, were completely unintelligible to us. It was our first *decima*, the verses of which were directed at us as a welcome. The fierce gentleman turned his attention to each of us in turn, blasting away in what resembled an outraged upbraiding. Feijoo explained that it was a statement of the profound kindness the three of us had done the people by paying their beloved Cuba a visit.

We visited Pasocaballo, a resort hotel on the blue, blue bay a short distance from Cienfuegos. It was new. It had been built as a worker's vacation spot. Hundreds of workers and their families were spending their vacation there. It was a rather plain hotel. There were none of the frills of the Riviera, our hotel in Havana. Each room had a balcony and plain comfortable cots, a sort of semibath with paper bathmats, and a toilet and shower. The food was nothing special, but it was plentiful once the waiters in their frayed tuxedos and black patent-leather bow ties finally delivered it to our table.

It was at Pasocaballo that I found out that Russian TV must be the world champion most boring being produced anywhere. In a corner of the vast lobby sat a big TV set that ran Russian-made TV soap operas of the sappiest sort, and nothing else, hour after hour.

It was there, too, that I discovered that telephone calls only cost a nickel in Cuba. They started out being free, but teenagers kept the phone tied up for so long every day that the government put on the nickel charge to discourage abuse. A telephone worker vacationing there passed this bit of information.

During the short time that we were in Cuba we managed to see a great many places and people. For several days Fred and Wendy walked the streets of Havana, photographing in bars, schools, markets, restaurants, barber shops, buses, dock workers' canteens—all the places where the ordinary people of Cuba functioned. For the most part I went along with them, taking notes. We were on our own, and not once did anyone challenge what we were doing there or even ask for our credentials. The people we talked to were open, direct, and friendly—eager to tell us about their work and their revolution. Pride was their most obvious attribute.

We spent several evenings with Cuban intellectuals, filmmakers, photographers, playwrights, and musicians; and had some open, freewheeling discussions on what might happen in Central America. They were deeply concerned.

We left Cuba not as experts on Cuba, but at least having seen enough of life there to use our experience as a backdrop to gauge the reaction of people to whom we spoke after our return to the United States. It seems regrettable to me that the reaction of our friends, when we speak about Cuba, ranges from indifference to hostility. People seem distressed to hear that the Cubans are not starving and that there is no unemployment. They seem pleased when I tell them that the housing situation in Cuba is terrible, that what clothing there is in the stores is shabby and expensive. They smile and nod knowingly when I tell them that the official newspaper *Granma* is rather boring reading, laden as it is with party propaganda. They seem pleased to learn that life in Cuba is still rather spartan.

For some reason it seems to upset some Americans greatly when I tell them that from what I observed, the people seem to love Fidel, that the ice cream is fantastic, and that medical services are good and available to everyone; that doctors are plentiful and free.

It seems obvious that the interests of the American people are best served by accurate, rational information. It is just a matter of common sense that it is not in our interest to have a distorted, false picture of a nearby neighbor, like the one we have maintained so long of Cuba.

X
A Little Fiction

X

The Man Who Knew Lyndon Johnson

My sister Mary called me a couple of weeks ago and said, "Johnny, since you like to get anecdotes that show insight into great people, you should go see Miss Mattie Matthews who lives down on the county line between here and the Driftwood Road. She has the most remarkable story about Lyndon Johnson as a young man, because she lived over in San Marcos when he went to Southwestern State Teacher's College. You really ought to go see her."

So I drove down there and sure enough found her place, a house about a hundred and fifty feet off the county road. There were oleanders along her gravel walk, and Miss Mattie Matthews was sitting up on her porch on a swing. She was just as friendly and hospitable as she could be, even though I had never laid eyes on her before, when I told her why I had come.

"Yessirree honey, I can tell you that story about Lyndon Johnson. And I wouldn't mind telling it, neither, because it's true. Now if it was just idle gossip you couldn't pry it out of me with a crowbar. Nossirree, I don't traffic in gossip and I won't sit and listen to it. The Bible's against it and I'm against it. I believe in the truth and if I didn't know this firsthand, you couldn't get it out of me.

"Course I never knowed Lyndon face to face. But my nephew Gervis used to fish with a one-armed fellow named Woodrow Wilson Haynes up there on the Blanco River. That Woodrow Wilson—I don't know how he lost his left arm. It was either in a hay mower or in a car wreck, or it could have been jerked off by an alligator. I'll say this for Woodrow Wilson Haynes, being one-armed that way didn't keep him from having eight children and every one of them had two arms and two legs when they was born, and they growed up that way, too.

"That oldest boy of his, Melvin Haynes, married Mattie Knox down there between Bastrop and Creedmoor. She was the widow of Frank Knox, you know, that got struck by lightning. He was riding a mule and it broke his back and the mule's hip when the lightning struck, or else it was his hip and the mule's back. It must have been Frank's back because he died. Of consumption. About a week later.

. .

"Well, his sister had a stepson that went to school with Lyndon. That's how I know. Gervis wouldn't have told a story, honey. Gervis was awful honest. Everybody in his family was that way. It was his sister, now, who married Fred Sassman. You know, they run Sassman's gin out there close to Dessau. I say run it—he run it one Saturday morning and he fell into it and ginned hisself into a bale of cotton.

"He was six-and-a-half foot tall, but when he come out in that bale of cotton he wasn't over a foot and a half long, they estimated. They never did *see* him, because she wouldn't let them take him out. You know, that's how her and Brother Wilkie had such a falling out down at the funeral parlor. Brother Wilkie wanted to pull Fred out and put him in a coffin, and she said let's bury him in the bale of cotton, it's just as good a coffin as he'll ever get. And she did. It hurt Brother Wilkie's feelings. Well, I can understand, see, an undertaker makes his money out of coffins, don't he? If that trend kept up, he could go plumb out of business.

"Brother Culpepper came down from Liberty Hill to preach the funeral, of course. Now there was a cutter for you. He was the only Culpepper that ever took to the church, but when he was called to preach, the old Methodists and Baptists got as bad as the labor unions. They won't ordain you unless you can read and write, so Brother Culpepper said, well, he didn't know that Jesus spent all his time a-studying and so, the hell with it, honey, he ordained hisself. Set up his own preaching and was good at it, too. And he was inventive. God called on him to invent for sick people and shut-ins a Do-It-Yourself Baptismal Kit, called Culpepper's Delight. It was interdenominational: it would sprinkle you or immerse you, and fit any religion. He sold it through the mail order for $4.98. If you sent your money ahead, you got an extra bonus. An autographed picture of Jesus Christ that glows in the dark. His oldest daughter, Mabel, broke his heart, though.

"She married a Methodist, Sam Rice from up at Round Rock. His daddy, Herman Rice, was a big Methodist, a full-blooded one. He had that big old collie dog named John Wesley, and you know that dog's a Methodist, too. People say Rice trained that dog to bite Baptists. I never did believe that. I don't think a dog could tell the difference between a Baptist and a Methodist. Catholics, yes, I could see that, but I don't believe Baptists and Methodists. It was Herman Rice's niece Bertha that had such hard luck as far as raising children was concerned. Don't know if you remember how she lost her first baby. Bertha took that sweet little six-week-old baby to the circus. She was standing there with that baby in her arms watching a great big old elephant eating peanuts. That old elephant was swinging his snout and reaching out and getting peanuts from folks. All of a sudden, without so much as a howdy-do, he reached right over with that old snout, plucked that baby out of Bertha's arms, tucked it into his mouth, and swallowed it whole. And he just stood there like nothing had happened, waving his old snout and fanning his ears. It upset Bertha something terrible. She ain't been back to a circus since.

"Honey, what time have you got there on your watch . . . oh my gracious, three o'clock. There's Betty Mae Harrell now, coming to get me. We're going down to Lockhart for a funeral. I don't know who the corpse is, but I missed the last two they've held and I ain't going to miss this one.

"Now I want to tell you all about Lyndon Johnson, so if you've got some time on your hands one of these days, you come by. I'd just love to tell you that story. And as I say, it's true, or I wouldn't fool with it."

Old Man Moss

You could see old man Moss's place easy from the county road that runs over to Walnut Springs. But you never did. His little old grey-brown house sat there among the pin oaks in plain view, but somehow you never did see it. I don't know why. It was just one of those things that has been there all your life, but that you never do think about looking at until somebody points it out to you. And it was the same way with old man Moss. You never did notice him, either. Lots of the folks around in this part of the county knew him, that is, they would tell you they knew him, but not a single one of them had ever talked to him, or really looked at him.

I don't guess that anybody had talked to him or even thought about him since the last one of the Lewis girls died 'way back around 1900. The Lewises had always sort of looked after him. Papa can remember when they built him that little house and deeded him a couple of acres of sandy land. Old lady Hiram Lewis had that done. You see, old man Moss had been sort of adopted by the Lewises 'way back before the Civil War. I'd be willing to bet that he hasn't said half a dozen words to nobody since the last Lewis girl died.

Like I say, old Man Moss was just like that little old grey-brown house of his. It seemed that you never noticed seeing him. He would just come walking into town about once a month with a sack of potatoes and some eggs to swap for matches or salt or cornmeal up at Franklin's store. He never stood around and yarned with folks like most people do. He would just take his things and go walking back out the road toward his place. I reckon he would have died without a person in this county being able to tell you just what he looked like, if it hadn't been for the big centennial doings we had here.

A couple of dressy, pleasant-looking young fellows came out from Austin. They signed up a contract with the county centennial committee to put on a sure-enough big-time celebration for the whole county. They were the sort of fellows that make it a business to go around and work up big to-dos like we were fixing to have. And I'll have to say right here that them two fellows beat all I ever saw. They got everybody interested in that celebration.

They are the ones that found out about old man Moss. They were looking around in some old records up at the courthouse and found out that old man Moss was the oldest citizen in the county. Well, sir, they sure did play that up big. It even got in the Austin papers. The folks around town were sort of puzzled. You would hear them saying, "Well I declare! Old man Moss! Why I know him, that is, I know who he is. The oldest man in the county! Now don't that bang bobtail!" And they would wag their heads and kind of laugh.

A couple of mornings after they found out about old man Moss, the two young fellows and a couple or three newspaper reporters and photographers from Austin came into my place. I was chairman of the centennial committee and they wanted me to go out to old man Moss's place with them. I had an idea that they were going to be asking a mighty lot of questions about history and the county that I couldn't answer. So I told them that we had better go up to the schoolhouse and get Miss Lovey before we started. I figured that she could answer all their questions. She knows more about history than anybody I ever saw. She can straighten you out in a hurry on any question that it takes book learning to answer. She likes for folks to know that she reads all the time.

We got Miss Lovey, and while we were on our way out there, the reporters started asking questions about old man Moss. I couldn't tell them a thing. I got sort of tickled at Miss Lovey. She'd been used to answering any question that a person would pop at her, but she couldn't tell them a thing about the old man. I could tell it sort of got off with her.

When we got to his place, we saw a little trail running off the side of the road to a hole in the fence. Old man Moss never had put a gate up. He just crawled through the fence when he was going to or from town. We did the same and followed the path toward his house. It ran through the weeds and then a patch of black-eyed peas to the yard. Around the house the yard was plain and bare. It wasn't shabby looking, but it didn't look fixed up. The house was the same way. It had the sort of grey-brown look about it that houses get when they haven't been painted in years and years. There wasn't anything ugly about the place, nor pretty either. It just reminded you of the sky when the clouds are high and grey on a cool fall day.

Old man Moss was sitting in a straight-back chair on the front porch when we walked up. He just sat there and sort of nodded at us. One of the young men, who had a cheerful voice and was always smiling, called out, "Hello there, Mr. Moss, I'll bet you weren't expecting company today." And then he laughed. Old man Moss shook his head and said, "No, I can't say that I was." From the way he acted you would have thought that we walked up like that every week.

The young man asked him in a sort of joking way if he realized that he was one of the county's most distinguished citizens. The old man said, "No." Then the young man told him that we had come out to inform him that he had the honor of being the county's oldest citizen. Old man Moss nodded. The young man looked sort of taken aback by old man Moss's just nodding, so Miss Lovey stepped up. She told the old man that our county was fixing to celebrate its one hundredth birthday and that we wanted him to celebrate it with us. He nodded. She told him that we would like to honor him by having him sit on the platform when the governor and other important people spoke. Old man Moss nodded. She asked him if we could persuade him to say a few words at the celebration. He nodded. Then she made a sort of speech on our old pioneer stock and the great empire that they had wrested from the savage and the wilderness. She ended up by saying that it meant a lot to her to stand before one of the men that had helped capture the frontier and make Texas what it was today. Old man Moss just looked at her and sort of nodded.

Then the reporters started in on him. They asked him if he remembered the Civil War. He said that he remembered the time it was fought, but that he had never seen any of the soldiers or anything connected with it. They asked him if he could remember when there were Indians in the county. He said he had heard of them, but had never seen any. They asked him if he could remember when the great herds of cattle were driven up the trails. He said he'd never seen one. They told him that they guessed he was one of the last links with the county's colorful past. Old man Moss nodded.

The photographers asked him if they could take some pictures of him. He said, "Yes." They took pictures of him standing up and sitting down and then standing up and holding a book of Texas history with Miss Lovey. When they were through, he sat back down in his chair, and we left.

The big celebration was held on a Saturday. Folks came into town from every direction. We had two high school bands, the American Legion band, and the Shrine band. When one wasn't playing, another one was. The courthouse square was roped off and the speakers' platform all wrapped in red, white, and blue cloth. Besides the governor and four or five other speakers, the whole centennial committee was on the stand. Old man Moss was sitting up there, too, not one bit disturbed by the crowd. In fact, to look at him sitting there, you would have thought he had been sitting on speakers' platforms all his life.

The children from the Medford Independent School District sang a song. Then all the bands joined together and played, "Beautiful, Beautiful Texas," while the crowd sang. The next number on the program was a prayer by Brother Harrell, the Baptist preacher. I noticed that while he was praying, old man Moss didn't bow his head like most folks did. He just sat there and looked like he didn't care whether they were praying or not.

The governor was the first speaker. He made a talk on the Alamo and the blood-drenched shrines in Texas and the glorious heroes that had died so that we could live in the greatest state in the United States. He would almost cry when he talked about heroes and sacrifices. The folks clapped and cheered for a long time after he finished.

Judge Hanes was next. He spoke awful flowery on the part our county had played in the growth of Texas. Then he sort of broadened out on the part our county had played in the growth of the whole United States. The folks clapped and cheered when he finished.

Miss Lovey was going to introduce old man Moss. She started out her speech by telling how bloodthirsty Indians had once roamed the county, plundering and murdering where quiet homesteads now stood; how the boys in grey had marched off to fight in the Civil War from this very county; how fearless cowboys had gathered and driven cattle up the trails from our county; how the county had seen the most dramatic part of Texas history and had done its part in the making of the great empire. Then she said that those days were gone forever, but that the spirit and flavor of those glorious days still lived in the person of one who had seen it all and been part of it. She said that the county should be proud to honor one who had been so much a part of those stirring times, one who had been a faithful, loyal citizen longer than anyone in the county, Mr. Joe Moss.

The crowd clapped and cheered. A fellow on the platform jumped up to help old man Moss to his feet, but he had already walked up to the front of the stand. When the folks had quieted down, old man Moss said in a plain, natural voice, "I have lived here in this county all my life." And then he walked back to his seat and sat down. The folks clapped and cheered for a long time.

After the speaking was over, the governor went over and shook hands with old man Moss and said something funny. Lots of other folks went over and shook hands with the old man. Then he got down from the platform and went walking out the road toward his place.

Teedy Was a Lady

Ordinarily, I can take pronouncements from Washington or leave them. However, the other morning about daybreak I was listening to three poultry experts from the Department of Agriculture in Washington hold forth over the radio, and they made certain statements about hens that I cannot let go unchallenged. They were discussing the care and feeding of laying hens. In positive flat tones, they seemed to agree that hens were useful only as producers of eggs or as dressed poultry. Well, it so happens that they are 'way off base there. My mother, no mean authority on hens herself, once held that opinion. I participated in a drama that proved her—and the experts—forever wrong, and as far as I am concerned placed hens well up the scale in acumen and wit.

You see, I have known some hens in my day, known them well. Mama kept a flock of brown leghorn hens that were as shrewd and alert on the whole as a class of Bryn Mawr seniors. I remember in particular one hen, Teedy. As a matter of fact, I think that it is my memory of Teedy that has me so incensed at the experts from the D. of A.

Teedy, with golden eyes, bright red comb, and soft brown feathers, had wit and originality. And Teedy did what I dared not do, particularly at the time she came into my life. (I was ten years old.) She flaunted Mama's rules. I think this latter action on Teedy's part is the thing that keeps her memory something of a beacon in my childhood.

Mama managed her family, the affairs of the local Methodist church, and her henhouse with a sure, firm hand. She had some eighty brown leghorn hens that she fed and sheltered well. She asked only one thing in return from them: each hen was expected to lay an egg at reasonably regular intervals. This was something of a hard and fast rule, and the hen that did not obey it to the egg was served up with dumplings at our Sunday dinner. The hens seemed to sense this. When Mama walked into the chicken yard, a sort of respectful silence fell over the flock, somewhat like the atmosphere that prevails in a barracks full of G.I.'s when the First Sergeant passes through.

There was only one exception to Mama's must-lay rule. When a hen wanted to "set" instead of lay, Mama would grant her several days' reprieve to get over her silly notion. We maintained a sort of correction coop for such offenders. When we discovered a hen ruffled and clucking on the nest (the sure sign that she had been seized with the desire to set), Mama would command me to place her in the correction coop. There the hen would cluck and fuss, ruffling her feathers and giving herself the airs of a setting hen for a few days, then give in. The process of placing her in solitary confinement to frustrate her maternal instincts was called "breaking her up." The signal that she had successfully been broken up and was ready to return to her duties in the henhouse was given by her ceasing to cluck and ruffle up her feathers, setting-hen–style. Of course, it did not have to be that way. One could take a setting of fertile eggs and place them under the setting hen and let her fulfill her natural inclinations. But Mama never did. She bought her baby chicks from a nearby hatchery. She had no desire to have her hens waste time setting on eggs. She wanted them to lay or get off the nest, as it were.

One sunny afternoon in late spring, Mama called to me as I was busy fashioning a slingshot from a forked cedar limb, "Johnny, there's an old sister trying to set out there in the henhouse. Get her and put her in the coop. I want to break her up." I trotted out to the henhouse and looked in the various nests for the offender. All of the regular layers were long since through for the day and were pecking about at the grain that Mama had just thrown to them. The setter was located in a nest, and as I approached her she greeted me with ill-humored clucks and testy passes at my hand with her beak. I had a third-grade schoolteacher at that time, who that very day had given me several sharp thumps on the head for having violated one of her innumerable rules. The hen's general appearance and disposition so closely resembled that of Miss Teedy that I named her "Miss Teedy" on the spot. I fenced and maneuvered with her until I got one hand firmly around her ruffled neck. I ran the other hand under her warm body and seized her legs. Grasping her thusly, I bore her to the prison coop, her golden eyes flashing fury and indignation.

Mama was never one to shilly-shally around with sentimentality where setting hens were concerned. The correction coop was barren of even a roost. The culprits had to squat on the ground. They were subject to a rigid diet of grain and water. Most of them fumed for a few days at the injustice of it all and were then ready to go back to laying. But Teedy was still just as markedly a setting hen after a week in the coop as she was the afternoon I fetched her from the nest. Mama took notice of this and said to me, "Johnny, that old sister is holding out too long to suit me." This was said within earshot of Teedy, but if she heard, she did not understand the implication, namely that she would push Mama too far and end up a Sunday dinner. At any rate, after another week she was still as waspish and fussy as ever. Mama was getting tired of this mutinous business, for she commented one afternoon near the coop, "I'll give that lady about two more days. If she hasn't given up by then, we'll have her for next Sunday's dinner." Miss Teedy regarded her with an indifference that amounted to outright defiance. By this time I had become somewhat fond of Teedy. I secretly admired her capacity to hold out against Mama. I found that I was actually distressed at the prospect of her becoming a Sunday dinner. As I was placing a pan of water in her coop later that afternoon, I confided to her, "Miss Teedy, if you've got it in you, lay. Mama means business. I know her." Teedy regarded me with what seemed to be a soft, friendly gaze. I had a sudden impulse to stroke her. I reached into the coop, and although she could have easily moved out of reach, she stood still as I smoothed down her pretty brown feathers.

I sat in front of the coop for some minutes, leaning back on my hands and working my bare toes through the wire of the coop, thinking. Miss Teedy pecked pleasantly at my big toe, and for the first time in nearly two weeks made the aimless ca-ca-ca sounds of a normal laying hen.

The next day Mama told me to put her back in the henhouse. She had laid that morning. I joyously returned Miss Teedy to the company of her feathered friends. But that very afternoon, as Mama came from gathering the eggs, she called, "Johnny, I do declare that I think that hen has gone back to setting. Anyway, she's on the nest. Put her in the coop." I went into the henhouse, and sure enough Miss Teedy was on a nest, as clucky and ruffled as the settingest of hens. I delivered her to the prison coop, with no protest whatever from her. As I slipped her into the coop, I felt bounden to tell her the dire consequences of her conduct. Mama would not give her even a week this time. If she did not overcome her urge to hatch out a brood, and settle down to the routine of laying, she would surely be sentenced to die by wringing of the neck. I secretly gloried in her spunk and determination. I so wanted her to win her point over Mama, but I trembled to think what grim end awaited her if she did not give up. I petted her and chatted with her for quite a while that afternoon.

I could tell by Mama's general demeanor when she came near the coop later that she regarded Miss Teedy with no little chagrin. As far as Mama was concerned, Miss Teedy had tricked her. She eyed the pretty hen with that silent disapproval that I had come to know so well when I used my Sunday school collection for ice cream at a confectionary instead of the collection plate. That look boded naught but real and present danger for its recipient.

But Miss Teedy laid the next day. Mama would never kill a laying hen, and although she almost hoped that Teedy would not lay, she ordered her back to the henhouse. The very next afternoon, however, Mama, without any attempt to conceal her indignant frustration, ordered me to "put that old sister back in the coop." Then, after a day or so, Miss Teedy presented us with another smooth white egg. I put her back in the henhouse once more. There she insisted on maintaining her status as a setting hen. For several weeks she was shifted to the prison coop and back into the henhouse every few days.

One afternoon, as I sat before the coop where the golden-eyed Teedy was imprisoned for about the tenth time, Mama came out and stood looking for a long time at the recalcitrant hen. I smiled, "Teedy laid again today, Mama." Mama drew her mouth into a firm, straight line. Eyeing Teedy balefully, she commented, "Well, tomorrow's Saturday. We're having Reverend Allen over for Sunday dinner. I think that we'll have chicken and dumplings."

"But Mama," I protested, "She's laying! Or sort of laying. She's trying to get over her settin'."

"I'm tired of fooling with her," Mama replied firmly. "She's carried this setting business just a little too far."

Long experience with that tone had taught me that further protest was pointless. After Mama went in the house, I sat by the coop in the late afternoon sun and talked to Teedy.

"I tried to tell you, Teedy. You wouldn't listen. Mama won't put up with your setting—I'm sorry. I'm awful sorry." If Teedy cared, she didn't show it. I patted her smooth neck feathers and she clucked pleasantly.

As I started into the house, I suddenly remembered something dreadful. I was the official executioner in the family. Wringing a chicken's neck had never bothered me in the least. It always struck me as the quickest, surest way to send a chicken to the hereafter. My sisters were repelled by the act. So was my father. So Mama and I were the only neck-wringers in the family, and Mama would be busy getting ready for Sunday! It would fall my lot to wring Teedy's neck! I was smitten with horror.

Mama was pressing butter into a butter mold when I went into the kitchen.

"Mama, let's don't kill that hen. She'll go back to laying regular."

"What on earth are you talking about?" Mama glanced at me, amazed at my sudden interest in the poultry business. "Nobody in this family likes chicken and dumplings better than you do!"

"Yes, but can't we eat another chicken? Why does it have to be Teedy?" I was urgent.

"Because she won't give up that notion she has to set! You know that!" Mama sounded perplexed by my even raising a question about Teedy's coming fate. I despaired.

At that moment, the phone rang. It was Mrs. Brodie. She had put a setting of eggs under a hen the past week. The hen had deserted the nest. Did Mama by any good fortune have a hen that was setting at the moment?

Mama replied in the affirmative.

XI
To Secure the Blessings of Liberty

In this speech, delivered before the National Convention of Professional Journalists in 1980, John Henry Faulk recounts his experiences in fighting the blacklisting of the 1950s—and winning. It was "scoundrel time," as Lillian Hellman has called it, and Faulk's victory with attorney Louis Nizer was a lamp showing the way out of the darkness. Faulk's major theme was developed in those long years of his lawsuit in the early 1960s: that fear and ignorance are the greatest dangers to civil liberties in our country.

At the age of eleven, I became a Texas Ranger and rode the frontier with a sidekick of mine named Tom Sikes, establishing law and order and protecting the weak from the depredations of outlaws. It was that part of the Texas frontier that stretched from Mama's back door to our cow lot. We did it on stick horses with rubber guns. Long before the Pentagon even dreamed of body counts, we'd stack up dozens of outlaws after just one skirmish in the morning out around the henhouse.

One morning Mama called out the door, "Would you mighty lawmen go out to the henhouse? There's a chicken snake in one of the hen's nests out there. Get a hoe and dispatch it."

We galloped up—we were both barefoot and in overalls—and charged into the henhouse. The hens were in a state of acute agitation. Tom and I began to look in the hens' nests. Mama's nests were in tiers of three. The top tier was a little too high to look into. About the fourth nest we peeked into, a chicken snake peeked back at us.

Now, I don't know how many of you have ever viewed a snake from the distance of six inches from the end of your nose, but although it's the size of your little finger, it takes on the proportions of a boa constrictor. All of Tom's and my frontier courage drained out our heels, or, rather truthfully, trickled down our overall legs.

Tom and I made a new door through the henhouse wall. Mama came out to see what was going on and said, "Lord have mercy, I thought I was protected. You've lulled me into a false sense of security here. You two mighty lawmen have let a chicken snake run you out of the henhouse. Don't you know a chicken snake is harmless and can't hurt you?" Tom, rubbing the seat of his britches and his forehead at the same time, said, "Yessum, Miz Faulk,

I know that, but they can scare you so bad, hit'll cause you to hurt yourself!"

I thought that might be a good topic to talk to you about today. I want to talk to you about what happens to a people who were conceived in liberty, whose original documents deal with the love of liberty, who proclaimed liberty as the cause of fighting what is now known as the Glorious Revolution—what happens to such a people when they become so frightened at the guaranteed constitutional freedoms that uphold that liberty, that they turn and trample them in panic.

Thirty years ago, this country was in just such a tailspin. A carefully manipulated and orchestrated wave of hysteria and fear was sweeping over the land, originated and augmented by such engines of repression as the House Un-American Activities Committee and the Senate Committee headed by Senator Joseph McCarthy. They could hail schoolteachers, professors, and ministers of the gospel before them and hold an inquisition to examine them for their beliefs and associations in complete and total contradiction to the spirit and the word of the First Amendment.

An outfit called the Federal Bureau of Investigation, headed up by J. Edgar Hoover, made it its business to surveil the political beliefs and associations of the American people. To publicly criticize it was to get into trouble. The FBI and its methods proliferated everywhere. Vigilante groups, wrapping themselves in red, white, and blue with the Bible under one arm and a flag in the other, proclaimed they were going to protect the people from the dread communist conspiracy that had its bony hand on the throat of the White House. The power of this hysteria ran right up through the government. We lived under "twenty years of treason." The Democratic Party was even called the party of treason.

The wave of fear played mischief with the political dialogue in this land—the lifeblood of our system. That's what the whole period of repression was about, shutting off the dialogue.

I was in the radio and television industry in New York. I was choppin' in the tall cotton. I had been carried up to New York by CBS as a folk humorist right after World War II. Of course, you must understand that that period was the time when we were launched in the atomic age. Willy-nilly, we had wiped two cities off the face of the Earth. This made man stand back and gasp. We had moved into the age of instant communication around the globe and intercontinental travel by supersonic air speeds. There was a vast uneasiness that ran through the whole land. A wave of political opportunism seized on this advantage. You might as well face the truth that the Republican Party rode to victory in 1952 on a wave of anticommunism.

There had been organized in the radio and television industry in New York an organization called AWARE, Incorporated. It had as its stated purpose to combat the communist conspiracy in the communications industry. That presumes two things: that there *was* a communist conspiracy in the communications industry, and that AWARE was the proper and authorized group to combat it. I accepted neither one of those presumptions.

I lived along Madison Avenue. I knew that the mentality there was to sell soap and underarm deodorant and nothing else—certainly no ideas of any kind. At the same time, it was my understanding of our Constitution that when you saw evidence of a crime being committed, you were obligated to take that evidence to the proper authorities. The person should be confronted with the charges, be allowed to bring witnesses, and be guaranteed due process of law.

Well, that ain't the way AWARE done their business, children! AWARE combatted this communist conspiracy by publishing a list of names and circulating it to the executives of the radio, television, and advertising agencies and sponsors. That list named persons who had, maybe ten or twenty years earlier, signed a petition, marched in a parade, spoken before a group, or entertained at a party under circumstances AWARE had decided suggested less than a loyal persuasion to the United States. The networks and agencies and advertising sponsors were queried, "Do you want to be a part of the international communist conspiracy? Please let us know by return mail what you intend to do about these persons."

It's not particularly a matter of rejoicing to say that they all responded by firing the persons listed. They never called them in and asked, "Is this true or false?" The networks didn't want to get involved.

In the first place, no one who was accused in this way was ever charged with any violation of the law, or the commission of any crime whatsoever. They were charged with having associated with, or having thought, the wrong ideas. These people were entered on what was called a "blacklist." They became untouchables.

It was a dread period because dear and fine friends of mine had their careers totally smashed and destroyed. Some actually were driven to suicide because, you see, it was as Garry Moore said, "It was like being in a dark closet being hit by five different men and not knowing from where the blow was coming."

It was a desolate period. The engines of repression rode high. To publicly criticize the blacklisters, to sign a petition for the abolition of the House Un-American Activities Committee, was to bring on blacklisting. To publicly criticize J. Edgar Hoover was unthinkable.

We belonged to a union called AFTRA—American Federation of Television and Radio Artists. It was a closed shop. You had to belong to the union to perform on network radio or television. I began to ask questions that were making me uneasy. Why wasn't AFTRA doing anything to stop blacklisting? I began to feel a bit unclean. I remembered my Daddy in the battle with the Ku Klux Klan one time in Texas. The Klan had burned a cross on the St. Edward's University campus in South Austin. Daddy, who was a lawyer, took them on, and was being congratulated by several folks for being courageous, because it was in the twenties when the Klan was riding sky-high. Daddy had said, "That isn't a matter of courage. That's a matter of responsibility as a Methodist layman and as a citizen of this country. I have a duty. You don't congratulate a man for doing his duty."

Well, that began to burn and work at me. I was sitting watching the engines of repression going full steam that could destroy the very fabric of this republic that has given such hope to mankind through the last 150 to 175 years.

Some of my fellow entertainers and I got to talking about why the union didn't do something about this terrible business of blacklisting. One of the union members said, "Don't you know, you can't go to a union meeting. The board of directors of the union is the board of directors of AWARE. That's how they control this union. It's pro-AWARE. It's problacklisting."

I got up and made a speech on how we weren't founded by cowards and shan't be saved by cowards. Gentlemen, I concluded, let's run in our own candidates and wipe them out. And we did. They "jined" me, and at the next AFTRA election, we swept them out of office. That was in 1955—made front page in the newspapers—the first antiblacklist slate that had taken over the union. Don't confuse this union with SAG—the Screen Actors' Guild. Ronald Reagan was president of SAG, and at that time they were all for blacklisting.

There we were, officers of AFTRA and none of us had ever been to a union meeting. A week later the House Un-American Activities Committee sounded the alarm by issuing a press release that the reds had moved back into the entertainment industry. A group of reds under the false banner of antiblacklisting had taken over AFTRA, the committee claimed.

Two weeks later AWARE put out a bulletin saying, this slate of officers who call themselves anticommunist is due some examination from good anticommunists. Let's take a look at Faulk who heads it up. He says that he is not a communist. Let's look at his record. Then they published several items relating to activities of mine in the past.

They said that according to sworn testimony before the House Un-American Activities Committee, John Henry Faulk was a speaker at a dinner at the Astor Hotel in 1947 under the auspices of a pro-communist organization with a man who has an unrepudiated record of communist activities.

Then I looked in my diary and sure enough, I was at the Astor Hotel that night in 1947. The item that AWARE left out was that this was the Year One birthday party for the Security Council of the United Nations. Indeed, there was a full-blooded, un-American communist named Mr. Gromyko savoring those capitalist vittles. Nor did AWARE mention that the cochairmen of the event were Mrs. Franklin D. Roosevelt and Mr. Harold Ickes, former secretary of the interior of the United States; nor did it state that the principal speaker at that gathering was the then-secretary of state Edward Stetenius; nor did it mention that CBS had sent me there because the program was being broadcast full network over CBS Radio. None of those items was mentioned, because this is the way AWARE operated—with its half-truths, distortions, and innuendos.

At any rate, I decided that this was a golden opportunity. I threw a suit on them. I got the most able lawyer I could find. I concluded that Mr. Louis Nizer was not only a genius in the courtroom, but that he also shared my sense of outrage at blacklisting.

It was made perfectly clear to me that I was placing my career on the line. I knew very likely it would change my whole course in life, and that I would probably lose some of the rooms in my apartment—maybe all of them. But the feeling of well-being and decency gave me a sense of genuine security.

We sued AWARE for conspiracy to destroy my career as a union

officer because I was threatening to expose their racketeering practices. You see, AWARE made a great deal of money out of fur-
nishing this information to the networks and agencies.

The suit was filed. We were off and running. I was absolutely
astonished at what fear does to people—I had not seen it firsthand
since the snake ran Tom and me out of the henhouse. People who
had spent time with me at my summer home, who were dear and
knew me well, became frightened and nervous to be seen with me
in public, despite our long friendship.

I established my position quite clearly in my own mind, and with
Nizer, when he asked if I had ever been a communist. I said, "No,
I'm not nor have I ever had an inclination to be, to answer you
perfectly candidly. But if I wanted to be, it would be my right as
an American citizen if that were my persuasion. That's the basis
for my taking on this fight. I think these fellows are a threat to our
republic. They're nothing more than fascists, as far as I'm concerned."

I discovered that people walking along Madison Avenue would
get across the street from me. I'd be embarrassed for their sake. I'd
walk into Toots Shors's, where I was very well known, and guys
would say, "Hi, John, I was just leaving."

CBS fired me and I was blacklisted, and couldn't earn a living.
My income went to zero. A lot of the people who were blacklisted
went to work in shoe stores and delicatessens, and tried to eke out
an existence. After trying several jobs that came to nought, I moved
down to Texas to hold on until the case came to trial.

It took five years to herd AWARE into the courtroom, but we
did it. Nizer had assembled the most astonishing library of wrongdoing on these people: the lives they'd smashed; the attitude they
took toward anybody who so much as blinked an eyelash in the
wrong direction; how they had literally run the hiring practice of
the radio and television industry. They had asserted their power
with complete arrogance.

The trial lasted three months. Mr. Nizer painted me in red, white,
and blue. While preparing me for my direct testimony, he'd gone
over my childhood carefully with me. The poor man was trying
to come up with something that would point up my virtue, but it
wasn't an easy task. I tried hard to think of some awards or honors
I had won or some acts that gave me distinction in the past. It was
slim pickings, I regret to say.

At the end of three months, Nizer absolutely dumbfounded me
by asking for $2 million in damages from the defendants. By this

time, the case had built to a real crescendo. All the people in the entertainment world who had been scarred and hurt—and that included almost everybody in it—were down there watching it. They had to move the case to a bigger courtroom, as a matter of fact. It was on the front pages of the papers all the time of the trial.

The jury went out. Newspapermen surrounded Nizer as we walked out, waiting for the jury to return. Nizer said, "If they come back soon, I think we've nailed this case down good and solid and we've put a stop to an awful, awful act of injustice. The whole country will owe this lone man here a great debt." Sure enough, here came a runner from the court. "The judge wants you back in court. The jury's coming back!" Nizer preened himself, "Well, I told you so. Let's go back in!"

We went back in and sat down. The judge said, "Mr. Foreman, have you reached a decision?" The foreman said, "No, we want to ask a question in the open court. May the jury give more than $2 million?" Well, Nizer looked as though somebody had caught him between the eyes with a ballpeen hammer. He had, I suppose, made mistakes in his legal career, but asking for too little had never been one of them. The jury went out and came back in less than thirty minutes with a $3.5 million judgment.

My loves, let me tell you something. No matter how long you've been plagued by aches, pains, and even congenital disorders, you let a jury stand up and pronounce that you've just won $3.5 million and it has a therapeutic effect on you.

I didn't get the $3.5 million. I got the reputation for having it because it was published—it was a record libel judgment at that time—in all the papers. There is nothin' calculated to scare kinfolks out of the woods like the news you just got $3.5 million. Take my word for that.

I got something far more important than money. I was being described by people whom I loved and respected as "courageous and heroic." I couldn't figure it out. Those are two attributes that are quite absent from my personality. It's just a fact. If there's a short in the lighting fixtures at home, I try to trick my wife into meddling with it for fear I might get shocked.

I was anxious to understand why a principled act was regarded as one of courage and heroism. I started to study what America really is. I started rereading history. I regard myself as a well-educated man. After all, I had gotten my master's degree at the University of Texas. I had worked on my doctorate. I had anticipated being an educator. I had minored in history.

I made an absolutely breathtaking discovery: I was ignorant of the real history and drama of who the American people are and what this republic really is. I started rereading the history of the American Revolution and reexamining 1776 and the forces preceding it. It's a breathtaking experience to read something we all take for granted, listen to all the time, and never reflect on: "When in the course of human events, it becomes necessary for one people to dissolve the political bands that have connected them with another, and to assume among the powers of the Earth, that separate, but equal, station to which the laws of nature and nature's God entitle them, a decent respect to the opinions of mankind requires that they should declare the causes that have impelled them to that separation. We hold these truths to be self-evident, that all men are created equal, and are endowed by their Creator with certain unalienable rights, and among these are life, liberty, and the pursuit of happiness. And that to secure these rights, governments are instituted among men, deriving their just powers from the consent of the governed."

This had never been pronounced before. The natural right that all humans are born with had never been made the basis for a struggle in that form. This changed the whole course of human history. I had never realized that the men who framed that statement went on to pledge their lives, fortunes, and sacred honor to achieving independence, although they represented less than a third of the colonies' population at that time. A third of the people were loyal British subjects and could hardly stand that old hippie crowd that George Washington assembled: a ragtail revolutionary outfit with Tom Payne running around printing those terrible things and handing them to the soldiers to keep them fighting. But they fell to and won that independence.

I never realized before that James Madison, a member of the Continental Congress from 1781 to 1787, was receiving boxes of books from Thomas Jefferson on the subjects of confederation, republics, and what part the church had played in tyranny. In 1787 Madison gathered with fifty-five of his neighbors in Philadelphia. Again for the first time in history, they sat down and began to frame a charter of government dedicated to the proposition that the people would be the masters and the government would be the servant, dedicated to the proposition that there would never be a religious test administered in these United States as a qualification for holding office, dedicated to the proposition that there would never be a state church or religion in this land. They were dedicated to the proposition that free men could govern themselves more adequately than could any other form of government.

In September 1787, they proclaimed to the world, "We the people of the United States, in order to form a more perfect union, establish justice, insure domestic tranquility, provide for the common defense, promote the general welfare and secure the blessings of liberty to ourselves and to our posterity, do ordain and establish this Constitution of the United States of America."

You and I are the posterity they believed in. By the same token, we are now "we the people." You will recall that when this remarkable document was sent out to the thirteen states to be ratified, the cry went up immediately, "It has no bill of rights! Our religious freedom is not guaranteed in that. Our right to speak our minds and to publish our beliefs is not sufficiently protected." The proponents of the new Constitution had to promise that the first thing they would do, if everyone would only go ahead and ratify it, would be to amend it and include a bill of rights that would assure those freedoms in perpetuity.

Sure enough, on June 8, 1789, during the First Congress, here came Congressman James Madison, saying, "I happen to have a list, gentlemen, that I've been instructed by the Virginia legislature to lay before you—some amendments to the Constitution." Some congressmen said, "Oh, let's do that next year. We're trying to get a government started here, Mr. Madison." He said, "No, you'd better act now or there won't be a government next year. The people are very jealous of these freedoms. They've had it with old King George and Lord North. They're not going to accept a federal government without these. You're just liable not to have a government next year."

The congressmen obviously concurred with him, because they sat down that year and debated the amendments. Until you've read the discussions that went on, you really can't understand the genius of this republic. James Madison, the man who wrote the First Amendment, described why he worded it as an absolute command and how he drew from the history of tyranny in Europe and understood it all so clearly. He said, "Congress shall make no law respecting the establishment of religion or prohibiting the free exercise thereof, or abridging the freedom of speech, or of the press, or the right of the people to peaceably assemble and petition their government for the redress of grievances."

This was my greatest gift from the struggle I had gone through.

I understood why James Madison conceived the First Amendment as the jewel in our crown, written and nailed into the basic law of the land, the guarantee that opinions we loathe and despise would be defended and protected with the same force as those we cherish and love. No other nation had ever dreamed of this. This *is* our genius.

I would remind you, my loves, of our great heritage that has been bestowed upon us by those men of imagination and wisdom, handed to us on a golden platter, the Bill of Rights.

This is our power and our strength. It has enabled us to confront the world as it really is, and to give us that kind of leadership at a time when Washington, D.C., is talking about a world that doesn't exist at all, at a time when people think you can use nuclear weaponry to solve the problems of the world. We are still a beacon the world looks to. It's up to you and me to use that power realistically and to assume again that role as a beacon for people from all corners of the Earth, the unwanted, the ones who sought a life of freedom. Respectability stayed at home, remember. Our ancestors came here looking for a richer life and found it.

How can people fight for and defend their freedoms in this land if they don't know what their guaranteed freedoms are? How can they be outraged at the fact that the Heritage Foundation is now seeking to reestablish the House Un-American Activities Committee, unshackle the FBI, and turn loose the engines of repression again, unless they know what their freedoms are?

This is our job: to open the dialogue in America. You are the people. You are America.